New International

A MAGAZINE OF MARXIST POLITICS AND THEORY

NUMBER 13   2005

Contents

ISSN 0737-3724
ISBN 978-0-87348-975-1
Manufactured in the United States of America

New International is distributed internationally by Pathfinder
Press: www.pathfinderpress.com

Cover design: Eva Braiman

Front cover: Top photo, coal-fired power plant in Didcot, England.
© Charles O'Rear/Corbis. Bottom photo, farmer near Bhena,
Nepal. © Macduff Everton/Corbis.
Back cover: Earth at Night, image by Craig Mayhew and Robert
Simmon, NASA, based on data from the Defense Meteorological
Satellite Program.

T̲AKE A LOOK at Earth at Night on our back cover. The shimmering clusters, faint patches, and dark expanses underscore the brutal class fact that a majority of the world's working people—largely in Asia, Africa, and Latin America—subsist without electricity or modern sources of energy, even for cooking and heat.

This composite of hundreds of satellite photographs is a stark measure of the huge inequalities, not only between imperialist and semicolonial countries but also among classes within almost every country, in social and cultural development and in the foundations for any sustained economic advance. These disparities, produced and accentuated every day simply by the workings of world capitalism, will widen further as competition for markets intensifies among the U.S. ruling families and their imperialist rivals in Europe and the Pacific.

Electrification "is an elementary precondition if modern industry and cultural life are to develop," Jack Barnes emphasizes in our lead article, "and communists fight for it to be extended to all—*all*—the world's six billion people. This fight is a prime example of how proletarian

3

politics, our politics, start with the world."

In order for class-conscious workers to build a world communist movement of disciplined proletarian parties, he notes, their week-by-week activity needs to be guided by a program, a strategy, to close—and then keep closed—these enormous economic and social disparities. Our job "is to make a revolution in the country where we find ourselves, where we live and work," Barnes explains. To accomplish that, "it's above all necessary for us to understand, and understand thoroughly, politics and the class struggle within those national boundaries.

"But we can do so only by starting with the fact that those national peculiarities and their changes are a product of the workings of a world market," he says. "We need to recognize that we are part of an international class that itself has no homeland—the working class—and to act always as though we are part of an international alliance with exploited and oppressed toilers throughout the world.

"That's not a slogan. That's not a moral imperative. It's not a proposed act of will. It is a recognition of the *class reality* of economic, social, and political life in the imperialist epoch." It is, Barnes says, an irreplaceable part of the activity of politically organized revolutionary workers, "the only force on earth that can carry out successful revolutionary struggles along the line of march of the proletariat toward political power."

"Our Politics Start with the World" was presented by Barnes, the national secretary of the Socialist Workers Party in the United States, to open a discussion at an international socialist conference held June 14–17, 2001, in Oberlin, Ohio. Among the nearly 400 participants were members, supporters, and friends of the Socialist Workers Party in the United States, the Communist Leagues in

Australia, Canada, Iceland, New Zealand, Sweden, and the United Kingdom, as well as dozens of Young Socialists and other workers, farmers, and young people from North America and elsewhere around the world. The following year "Our Politics Start with the World," edited for publication, was debated and adopted by delegates to the 2002 SWP national convention.

"Capitalism's Long Hot Winter Has Begun," the political report and summary by Barnes adopted by that same convention, together with "Their Transformation and Ours," SWP National Committee draft theses prepared by Mary-Alice Waters, editor of *New International*, are the featured articles in issue number 12 of this magazine. These companion issues, *New International* numbers 12 and 13, complement each other. "Capitalism's Long Hot Winter Has Begun," too, starts with the world. It centers on the accelerated contradictions—economic, social, political, and military—that have pushed the international imperialist order into the opening stages of a global financial crisis and depression, as well as a new militarization drive and expanding wars. This long, hot winter that world capitalism has now entered, Barnes notes, is one that "slowly but surely and explosively" will breed "a scope and depth of resistance not previously seen by revolutionary-minded militants throughout today's world."

The contents of these two issues of *New International*, published at the same time, are a contribution to the political preparations for that stepped-up and increasingly worldwide resistance by the toilers and their allies.

The wealth that makes possible human civilization and progress is, in its entirety, the product of social labor's transformation of nature, a labor that simultaneously transforms itself.

"Human labor is social labor," Barnes emphasizes in the closing remarks to the 2001 socialist conference printed here. "Its product is not the result of the work of an individual, nor even the work of many individuals summed together." The output of the labor of a farmer, a seamstress, a butcher, or a miner, he says, "is determined by the class relations under which they toil. It is social labor that bequeaths generation after generation the culture, the blueprints, to transform material reality in new and more productive ways and to make possible the creation of a better world." But, he added, as Marx taught us, so long as capitalism reigns, these improvements in the forces of production will simultaneously tend both to increase the intensification of labor and to produce more horrendous forces of destruction.

These questions of Marxist politics and theory, on which much of the discussion at the 2001 international socialist gathering focused, were the topic of one of seven classes organized for conference participants. The class was presented by Steve Clark, a member of the SWP National Committee. A few weeks later Clark used the presentation, enriched by the discussion at the conference, as the basis for preparing a four-part series in the *Militant*, a New York newsweekly published in the interests of working people worldwide. The series has been edited for publication here as a single article entitled, "Farming, Science, and the Working Classes."

"Capitalism, Labor, and the Transformation of Nature," an exchange between Richard Levins and Steve Clark, is the final item in this issue. Following publication of the articles by Clark in the *Militant*, Levins, professor of population sciences and a researcher at the Harvard School of Public Health, wrote a response. Levins is active in the July 26 Coalition, a Boston-area Cuba solidarity organization, and works with the Institute of Ecology and Systematics of the Cuban Ministry of Science, Technology and the Environment. Levins's article is published here for the first time, followed by Clark's reply and final comments by each author.

December 2004

OUR POLITICS START WITH THE WORLD

"Electrification is a precondition if modern industry and cultural life are to develop, Lenin pointed out. Communists fight to extend it to all the world's six billion people. This fight is a prime example of how proletarian politics start with the world."

TOP: Russian peasants study a map showing the electrification of Moscow, 1926. **BOTTOM:** Students in Cuba's Pinar del Río province celebrate installation of school solar panel, 2003. Revolutionary government has completed effort to ensure schools in remote areas have electricity and educational video programs.

Corbis

Ecosol Solar

OUR POLITICS START WITH THE WORLD

by Jack Barnes

I N DECEMBER 1920, the third year of the workers and peasants republic in Russia, V.I. Lenin made a statement that has often been repeated but less often understood. Speaking to the All-Russia Congress of Soviets, Lenin said: "Communism is Soviet power plus the electrification of the entire country."[1]

Since that day, any organization claiming to be communist has had to come to grips with that assertion. What connection does it have to the tasks of a revolutionary government fighting to consolidate workers and farmers power? What kind of clarity in thought and deed does it demand from a proletarian nucleus *well before the final revolutionary struggles through which the toilers come to power?* What do working people think of when they hear the name of the party, a communist party? What is it fighting for? Where is it heading?

The following is based on an opening talk and closing summary presentation at an international socialist conference in Oberlin, Ohio, June 14–17, 2001. Jack Barnes is the national secretary of the Socialist Workers Party.

FOOTNOTES BEGIN ON THE NEXT PAGE

Lenin's statement begins not with electrification but with *Soviet power*: the elected councils of workers, peasants, and soldiers whose meetings and decisions constituted the working-class power on which the new revolutionary government was based. But he doesn't stop there. To many at the time, and even more so eight decades later, it must have seemed that "Communism is Soviet power *plus* electrification" was an overreaching simplification. "That's Lenin, you know. As always, pushing a point a little too far." But Lenin, as always, was starting from a world view—from the concrete place of the workers and peasants of Russia as determined by the workings of the world imperialist system, its laws of motion. Not vice versa. Not the world as seen from Moscow or Petrograd. Not Russia somehow "fit into" the world.

LENIN, AGAIN AS ALWAYS, was also starting from the practical need to strengthen the alliance of workers and peasants, the two classes upon whose allied shoulders the dictatorship of the proletariat rested. The destiny of Soviet power was now inseparably intertwined with the advance of the struggle for national liberation and socialism throughout the world. What concrete steps were necessary to narrow the political gap between those two exploited classes, urban and rural? To narrow the gap in their conditions of life, their possibilities of education and culture, their political experience? How was it possible to narrow the gap in self-confidence, proletarian class consciousness, and political clarity? The differences in ability

---

1. V.I. Lenin, "The Eighth All-Russia Congress of Soviets" in Lenin, *Collected Works* (Moscow: Progress Publishers, 1966), vol. 31, p. 516. Hereafter *LCW*.

to politically understand, sacrifice for, and advance the proletarian dictatorship in Russia and extension of Soviet power to the world?

Lenin placed great store in the competent and disciplined use of technologies inherited from capitalism, as well as the skills of scientists and engineers willing to place their knowledge and training at the service of the Soviet republic. But what Lenin was raising was not a technical challenge, first and foremost. Nor was it primarily a military question, even though the strength of the worker-peasant alliance had just been put to the test of fire by the devastating human and material consequences of the civil war launched by Russia's capitalists and landlords, supported by the allied invasion of fourteen imperialist powers, including the United States. By late 1920, when Lenin presented the electrification plan, workers and peasants in Soviet Russia—and peasants made up more than 80 percent of the ranks of the Red Army—had defeated the counterrevolutionary forces.

The task now before the communist leadership of the revolution, Lenin said, was to lead these two classes in such a way that tens of millions, in both city and countryside, could see their conditions of life converging. Along that road the ground would be laid for the working class to become a larger and larger percentage of the toilers of city and countryside,[2] as well as for workers and peasants to more and more converge in political goals—to increasingly see the world, and their relationship with toilers' struggles in other countries, through a common pair of proletarian glasses.

---

2. In 1917 the population of the young Soviet republic was 140 million. Some 80 percent were peasants, and 10 percent were in the working class, including 2 million factory workers.

Only as this gap was narrowed could the working class learn how to organize to move beyond workers control of industry toward the management of production. Only as these divisions grew smaller could peasants see beyond the guarantees they had won to use the land they tilled and to obtain cheap credit, and move toward a broader perspective of the industrialization of the entire country that would progressively overcome the chasm between urban and rural life. The proletariat would consequently grow in size—in absolute numbers, as well as relative to the peasantry—and in political confidence. The alliance of the working class with the peasantry, and thus its class rule, would be strengthened and stabilized. With added confidence, the power of its example would increase. With added confidence, its offer of help to toilers worldwide would be extended and accepted more frequently, and carried out with greater success.

The use of equipment and machinery powered by electricity and internal combustion had to be widely extended to the countryside, Lenin said: "[W]e must prove to the peasants that in place of the old separation of industry from agriculture, this very deep contradiction on which capitalism thrived and which sowed dissension between the industrial and agricultural workers, we set ourselves the task of returning to the peasant the loan we received from him [during the civil war] in the form of grain. . . .

"We must repay this loan by organizing industry and supplying the peasants with the products of industry," Lenin underscored. "We must show the peasants that the organization of industry on the basis of modern, advanced technology, on electrification which will provide a link between town and country, will put an end to the division between town and country, will make it possible to raise the level of culture in the countryside and to overcome, even in the most remote corners of the land, backwardness, ignorance, poverty, disease, and barbarism."[3]

Lenin pointed out that without such a course, conditions in the young workers and peasants republic, especially in the countryside, would create and continually recreate layers of independent commodity producers who would face periodic crises and become increasingly differentiated economically. Easily convinced they were being betrayed by the proletariat, such layers would turn back to the bourgeoisie for leadership. That had become the greatest counterrevolutionary danger confronting the working class.[4]

Politically, the peasantry always follows one of the two major urban classes, either the capitalists or the working class. That fact is demonstrated by the entire history of the modern class struggle. So maintaining Soviet power depended on what might superficially seem to be a technical matter, a large-scale engineering project. But as Lenin emphasized, electrification of the country had to be understood and organized for what it was in history: a profoundly *political* question, the answer to which would determine, in life, whether the alliance of workers and peasants would rise or fall. Recognizing this task and aiding its realization was not simply a challenge for the toilers of Russia and their Bolshevik vanguard; it was a worldwide responsibility of communists, class-conscious

---

3. Lenin, "Report on the Work of the All-Russia Central Executive Committee," *LCW*, vol. 30, p. 335.

4. Lenin, "The Eighth All-Russia Congress of Soviets," *LCW*, vol. 31, p. 516.

workers, and revolutionary-minded farmers.

The communist party, Lenin said in his December 1920 report to the congress of soviets, has a political program that "is an enumeration of our objectives, an explanation of the relations between classes" in the young Soviet republic. But this party program "must not remain solely a program of the Party," he said. "It must become a program of our economic development, or otherwise it will be valueless even as a program of the Party. It must be supplemented with a second Party program, a plan of work aimed at restoring our entire economy and raising it to the level of up-to-date technical development. Without a plan of electrification, we cannot undertake any real constructive work. . . .

"Of course, it will be a plan adopted as a first approximation. This Party program will not be as invariable as our real Party program is, which can be modified by Party congresses alone. No, day by day this program will be improved, elaborated, perfected and modified,"[5] Lenin emphasized. It will be a task of workers and peasants in every workshop and in every rural area.

LENIN TOLD THE congress a story about visiting one of the first villages in Russia to be electrified. A peasant came forward to speak, welcoming the "unnatural light" that the new Bolshevik-led government had made possible. It was to be expected that rural toilers would initially look upon electricity as "unnatural," Lenin remarked. But what class-conscious *revolutionists* consider unnatural, he added, "is that the peasants and workers should have lived for hundreds of years in such backwardness,

5. Ibid., p. 515.

poverty and oppression under the yoke of the landowners and the capitalists."[6]

Everything that marks progress in the human condition is "unnatural" in that materialist sense—not just electricity but agriculture, livestock, handicrafts, and industrial products of every kind. None of these are directly appropriated from nature by individuals; all are the end result of human beings working together in a mesh of social relations. Every aspect of what we call civilization and culture is the product of the transformation of nature by social labor. (And we forget at our peril that we are at the same time *part* of nature, *part* of what is being transformed.)

What is unnatural has been the stunting of this potential for human development by social relations of exploitation, relations maintained through force of habit, supplemented by terror organized by the propertied classes. With the workers' and peasants' conquest of power, *their* government could finally organize to carry out what had been possible technically for several decades—that is, for toilers of both city and countryside to have electric light after the sun goes down. To have the option to extend the use of the day. To be able to decide whether to stop a meeting because it's getting dark. To have the possibility to study and work comfortably after sundown. For children to do their schoolwork or to read to each other in the evening. Simply to pump water to village after village, saving countless hours of back-breaking work for every family, and especially for women and girls.

The Bolsheviks' course was aimed at accomplishing something broader than the economic and social development of Soviet Russia. Lenin presented these perspec-

---

6. Ibid., p. 517.

tives on strengthening the worker-peasant base of Soviet power for discussion, debate, and adoption by the Third Congress of the Communist International, the world party of revolution founded in 1919 at the initiative of the Bolsheviks.[7] Without proletarian victories spreading to other countries, the socialist revolution in Russia would be hemmed in by the imperialist powers and defeated. This revolutionary perspective had to be fought for by an expanding worldwide alliance of workers and peasants, led by the communist workers movement.

Bridging the gaps among the world's toilers

The Bolsheviks understood that such a goal—workers of the world, unite!—was possible only if the conditions of the toilers on an international scale were converging. Only if this *cultural* gap was closing. Only if more and more working people across the globe were taking an active part in social and political life, and could thus recognize toilers engaged in such social activity elsewhere as their brothers and sisters, not simply see them as "the other." Understanding and then acting on this reality is the foundation of a citizen of the world.

The effort to electrify the entire country, Lenin said in the December 1920 congress debate, would go hand in hand with the "endeavor to stamp out illiteracy—but that is not enough. . . . Besides literacy we need cultured, enlightened

---

7. See "The Material Basis of Socialism and the Plan for the Electrification of Russia" in the "Theses for a Report on the Tactics of the R.C.P." drafted by Lenin, as well as his "Report on the Tactics of the R.C.P.," in *LCW*, vol. 32, pp. 459, 492–94. The latter report is reprinted as "A Very Unstable Equilibrium: Report on the Tactics of the R.C.P." in *New International* no. 12 (2005), pp. 278–90 [2011 printing].

and educated working people; the majority of the peasants must be made fully aware of the tasks awaiting us."[8]

At the opening of the twenty-first century, these questions, and others like them, remain at the center of building proletarian parties and a world communist movement. They remain central to the possibilities for concrete political collaboration and joint activity by working people in the battle for national liberation and socialism. This perspective is advanced by the growing size and social weight of the working class throughout Asia, Latin America, and expanding areas of Africa, as well as by every step to improve the economic and social conditions of urban and rural toilers—from electrification to literacy, from sanitation and potable water to access to modern medicine.

Our politics—proletarian politics—start with the world. That's not simply an accurate observation. Nor a snappy theme for a socialist conference. For all the reasons we've been discussing, it is a political necessity, the only place the working class *can* start and not end up in a swamp. In any one country, we are *not* more powerful than our own ruling class, much less the sometimes combined forces of several imperialist powers defending their world domination. A proletarian revolution has never triumphed and survived without international working-class solidarity powerful enough to affect the course of history.

It is the *proletarian* internationalism of communist politics above all that sets us apart from all bourgeois and petty-bourgeois forces. The intensifying rivalry of the imperialist rulers constantly drives them to every nook and cranny of the globe in the hunt for markets for their commodities and capital, as well as for sources of cheap labor

8. Lenin, "The Eighth All-Russia Congress of Soviets," *LCW*, vol. 31, p. 518.

and raw materials. In face of uprisings by the toilers and conflicts among themselves, they carve out international alliances and negotiate treaties to strengthen their respective positions, economically, politically, and militarily. But the world is not where they begin. Capitalist politics start with *their* borders, *their* currencies, *their* armed forces, *their* states—with bourgeois nationalism and patriotism in defense of their profits, prerogatives, and class rule.

Revolution, culture, and equality

In speaking of culture, communists today, like Lenin in 1920, do not mean only music and art, although that's encompassed by human culture. Nor does use of the word have anything in common with Stalinist cant (including its Maoist variants) about "cultural revolutions." These have always ended—after large-scale repression, even slaughter, of layers of "recalcitrant, backward" toilers and "intellectuals"—with the wanton and brutal destruction of cultural conquests and freedoms of which the working class is today the caretaker, protector, and champion. The "Cultural Revolution" under Mao Zedong in China, Pol Pot's extermination squads in Cambodia, and the course of Shining Path in Peru are among the horrors that come to mind from the past four decades. All followed in the trail blazed by Stalin. The banning of the science of genetics in the Soviet Union in 1948 is but one well-known example.[9]

---

9. Following the Stalinist regime's forced collectivization of the peasantry in the late 1920s and early 1930s, the combined effects of repression of rural toilers and their resistance to it led to a devastating drop in grain production. Hoping to reverse the disastrous consequences of its course, the regime latched onto the crank plant-breeding methods of Trofim Lysenko, in-

On the most fundamental level, *culture* is what distinguishes human beings from our most immediate two-legged ancestors in the millions-of-years-long evolution of primate life. What sets human beings off from the creatures that came before us is not the use of tools and tool-making per se, nor even the improvement of tools; both predate human beings by hundreds of millennia. What distinguishes human beings above all is the conscious social organization and planning to pass along knowledge of those improvements—their "blueprints"—to succeeding generations, and to build on those improvements.

Only human beings do that. That is the *unique* attribute of human labor in the evolution of our species and the origins and development of culture. That is the prerequisite of any progressive social transformation of nature at a pace more rapid than evolution could ever allow. That is the prerequisite, in the words of the Communist Manifesto, of the "constant revolutionizing of production" rooted in the birth of capitalism and its spread "over the whole surface of the globe."[10]

Culture is stunted, distorted, and corrupted within class society. Full access to the fruits of civilization is monopolized by the ruling layers. This monopoly is used as

---

cluding his opposition to the science of genetics. From the mid-1930s through the outright banning of genetics research and education in 1948, some eighty biologists, agricultural specialists, and others who resisted Lysenko's quackery were arrested, jailed, executed, or died in prison camps. A minimum of three hundred others were forced out of research or teaching jobs, and several scientific laboratories and institutes were closed down or "reorganized."

10. Karl Marx and Frederick Engels, *The Communist Manifesto* (New York: Pathfinder, 1987, 2008), pp. 34–35 [2010 printing].

an instrument to solidify the oppression and exploitation of the toiling majority, those whose social labor alone makes possible the advancement of culture. The triumph of revolutionary workers struggles aimed at overturning capitalist rule and the imperialist system initiates the battle to raise the cultural level of working people worldwide. Revolutionary victories open the road for us to transform ourselves, as we transform our social conditions. To become more immune to ruling-class demagogy aimed at rationalizing oppression and horrors of all kinds.

In a 1924 talk to a conference of Soviet workers' clubs, Bolshevik leader Leon Trotsky pointed out that for a peasant, culture may begin with "chemical crop-dusting methods for destroying locusts." For women, he added, it may begin with "public dining halls and nurseries [that] give a revolutionary stimulus to the consciousness of the housewife." In general, Trotsky noted, culture requires more than an increasing level of scientific, technological, and industrial development that "frees humanity from a dependence upon nature that is degrading." In addition, liberation from such conditions can only be completed when social relationships are "free from mystery," are "thoroughly transparent and do not oppress people."[11]

SUCH SOCIAL RELATIONSHIPS can only begin to be created with the revolutionary overturn of capitalist rule, establishment of workers and farmers governments, consolidation of the dictatorship of the proletariat, and the first steps in building socialism that this makes possible. That's

---

11. Leon Trotsky, "Leninism and the Workers' Clubs," in Trotsky, *Problems of Everyday Life* (New York: Pathfinder, 1973), pp. 407, 411 [2011 printing].

why, as communist leader Ernesto Che Guevara told medical students in Cuba in August 1960, "To be a revolutionary doctor, . . . there must first be a revolution."[12]

Well before the proletariat has replaced world capitalism with socialism, however, *political equality* begins to be forged within the revolutionary workers movement in the course of common struggle and mass work. That kind of equality is not limited to legal rights under a constitution. It's the opposite of bourgeois legal equality, which, while marking a historic advance over feudal arbitrariness, is stamped from its origins with the deformations of the social reproduction of class divisions.

In a bourgeois democracy we're all equal "under the law." During hard times early in the last century, socialist agitators used to recall the words of the French writer Anatole France: "The law, in its majestic impartiality, forbids the rich, as well as the poor, to sleep under bridges, to beg in the streets, and to steal bread." That's political equality today. It is an ideological rationalization for social relations that force workers, in order to survive, to sell our labor power to a boss who takes the product of our labor. It is a rationalization for the capitalist system that enriches a tiny handful of propertied families with the wealth produced by the labor of workers and farmers. It is a rationalization for the imperialist system with its inevitable tendencies toward intensifying competition of capitals; ruthless pillage of the semicolonial world; racist, religious, national, and anti-Jewish hatred; economic volatility and depression; social crisis; fascism (accurately called "national socialism"); and world war. It is used to

---

12. "To Be a Revolutionary Doctor You Must First Make a Revolution," in Ernesto Che Guevara, *Che Guevara Talks to Young People* (New York: Pathfinder, 2000), p. 52 [2011 printing].

rationalize all these products of capitalism with reactionary and learned opinion on the "backwardness" and "stupidity" of the producers at home and abroad.

Lenin and the Bolsheviks understood these class realities of bourgeois democracy in their bones, and set out to lead the workers to replace them worldwide.

Politics begin with millions

A successful revolutionary struggle for power opens the door to begin doing politics on a larger scale, and with greater consequences for the workers of the world. "Politics begin where millions of men and women are; where there are not thousands, but millions. That is where serious politics begin," Lenin reminded a party congress in March 1918.[13]

Néstor López Cuba, a division general in Cuba's Revolutionary Armed Forces, tells the story, recounted in *Making History*, of his initial response as a young Rebel Army combatant to the revolutionary victory in January 1959 over the U.S.-backed Batista dictatorship. He turned in his rifle and headed back to the family farm, telling his fellow combatants, "I'm off. The war is over." But his commander confronted him: "What? Are you chicken? How can you take off when things are just beginning?" López Cuba and hundreds like him stayed on to help lead the revolution.[14]

That's the point Lenin was emphasizing in his March 1918 report. After the working class has taken power, even

13. Lenin, "Extraordinary Seventh Congress of the R.C.P.(B.)," *LCW*, vol. 27, p. 100.

14. Mary-Alice Waters, ed., *Making History: Interviews with Four Generals of Cuba's Revolutionary Armed Forces* (New York: Pathfinder, 1999, 2000), pp. 23–24 [2010 printing].

more decisive challenges present themselves. Defense of the revolution is organized, proletarian internationalist consciousness of growing numbers of toilers is forged, and transformation of the conditions of humanity worldwide begins. That's politics.

What's more, it's the *final form* of politics in human history. There will be no politics after those goals have been achieved. It's difficult for us even to conceive of this today. Those of us at this conference are bending every effort to build the nucleus of mass parties and an international movement of professional proletarian politicians, soldiers of the revolution. To be political.

Communist workers need to recognize that the things we must do, the things that are so decisive to finally getting rid of what Marx and Engels called "the muck of the ages"[15] and the horrors of class society, involve using the best and the most up-to-date instruments inherited from that same old society. That is how the hereditary working class—still a new and growing class in the broad sweep of human history—can organize ourselves and other toilers to make revolutions in our own countries, overturn the imperialist system, and join in the worldwide struggle for socialism. That's the only way to open the road to a world without exploitation, without classes, without wars—and without the necessity of politics.

A few hundred years from now people will look back and need to have all this explained to them. What was "politics"? What was a "politician"? What were "soldiers"?

If we can begin to understand the centrality in revolutionary proletarian politics of bridging the cultural gap

---

15. Karl Marx and Frederick Engels, "The German Ideology," in *Collected Works*, vol. 5 (Moscow: Progress Publishers, 1976), p. 53. Hereafter *MECW*.

between the urban and rural toilers, not just in any one country but worldwide, then we can understand the alarm of the U.S. embassy in Cuba in 1959 when they reported to Washington how Commander Ernesto Che Guevara was using La Cabaña fortress in Havana. The captured garrison of the former Batista dictatorship was being used for military training of the Rebel Army. This was not the degrading and brutal hazing of new recruits that's standard procedure during basic training in bourgeois armies. Instead, along with discipline and growing skill in the use of weapons came the organization of literacy classes for rank-and-file soldiers and commanders, as well as poetry readings, art exhibitions, plays, concerts, and ballet performances. This was evidence, the U.S. operatives rightly argued, of the communist tendencies of the Cuban revolutionary leadership.

We can also better understand why the CIA directed the counterrevolutionary bandits in Cuba in 1961 to make the young literacy brigade volunteers special targets of terror. We should never forget the central priority Cuba's victorious Rebel Army and revolutionary government gave to a nationwide literacy campaign in the opening years after the victory. The effort had begun during the revolutionary war itself among the cadres of the Rebel Army, an army that came to be composed in its big majority of toilers from the countryside, many of whom could neither read nor write at the time they joined up. And in 1961, the Year of Education, the new workers and farmers government made the literacy campaign the galvanizing center of the revolution. Young people in their teens and early twenties, the sons and daughters of workers as well as those from the middle class in the cities, took a year off from their own classes or jobs in order to go live in rural areas and join in the battle to wipe out illiteracy. It was a countrywide battle to accelerate and make irreversible the possibilities opened for peasants and workers to seek, to acquire, and to use knowledge—the better to advance and defend the gains they were making.

What the young soldiers were learning at La Cabaña fortress, what youth across Cuba did during the literacy campaign—this was born of the same class consciousness and revolutionary proletarian solidarity that enabled Cuban working people to fight together and turn back the April 1961 U.S.-organized invasion at Playa Girón (what workers in the United States know as the Bay of Pigs). It is what enabled the Cuban toilers to stay Washington's hand during the October 1962 "missile crisis." It is the source of the political conviction, inspiration, and courage that has led hundreds of thousands of Cubans to volunteer for internationalist missions from Algeria, to the Congo and Angola, to Argentina and Bolivia, to Grenada and Nicaragua, Venezuela, and beyond. It is what accounts for the humane and principled character—the proletarian character—of Cuba's communist leadership from that day to this. What they began they have never stopped.

ALL THE QUESTIONS POSED by the ongoing crises and breakdowns of international capitalism can only be understood clearly, and answered in practice, if we start from a world perspective. Only then can we recognize and begin acting to advance proletarian alternatives, as opposed to the eternally recurring lesser-evil choices either of which reinforce the current social relations of exploitation and oppression.

The job of a communist party is to make a revolution in the country where we find ourselves, where we live and work. It's necessary for us to understand, and understand thoroughly, politics and the class struggle within those national boundaries.

But we can do so only by starting with the fact that those national peculiarities and their changes are a product of the workings of a world market. We need to recognize that we are part of an international class that itself has no homeland—the working class—and to act always as though we are part of an international alliance with exploited and oppressed toilers throughout the world. That's not a slogan. That's not a moral imperative. It's not a proposed act of will. It is a recognition of the *class reality* of economic, social, and political life in the imperialist epoch. That is what enables us to act effectively as Bolsheviks who are Americans (however temporarily), not as "American Bolsheviks." The latter may be aspired to by "well-meaning" boys and girls, as Trotsky once called the Shachtmanite youth who split from the proletarian party on the eve of World War II. But it is a form of national socialism just the same.

Electrification

As Lenin insistently pointed out, electrification is an elementary precondition if modern industry and cultural life are to develop, and communists fight for it to be extended to all—*all*—the world's six billion people. This fight is a prime example of how proletarian politics, our politics, start with the world.

That world perspective alone sets us apart from the imperialist ruling classes. It sets us apart from broad sectors of the petty bourgeoisies in the imperialist countries, who have been led to believe *they* have a right to *their* standard of living based on unlimited electrical power, but fear that its extension to billions of "others" would create "an unsupportable drain on natural resources," that is, a threat to their privileged conditions. And it sets the proletariat apart from the national bourgeoisies in the semicolonial world, whose electrification efforts are designed to power their needs, their business, commerce, and infrastructure, not schools and hospitals, homes and transport, water and sanitation.

Steve Clark looked up some figures on electrification in preparing the class he'll be presenting here at the conference. More than two billion people—one-third of the world's population—have no access of any kind to modern energy, either to electricity or to modern sources of fuel for cooking and heating. They must rely on candles or kerosene lamps for lighting, and on wood, dung, thatch, and straw for fuel. With no power for pumping, they rely on hand- or oxen-carted water supplies. The figure of two billion comes from the World Bank—a major imperialist institution—and likely understates the reality. For example, the World Bank itself points out that statistical bureaus in many countries, including India, "count all households in a village as being electrified if the village has one streetlight and one electric water pump"! If you live in many parts of today's world, of course, getting an electric water pump in your village, or an electric streetlight, is a red-letter day. But for the bourgeoisie to then claim those villagers have electrification is another matter.

The only parts of the world that come close to universal electrification, once again using World Bank figures, are the imperialist countries of North America, Western Europe, and Asia and the Pacific—that is, Japan, New Zealand, and Australia—as well as the workers states of Eastern and Central Europe and the former Soviet Union (including the Central Asian republics) and Cuba.

The gap we've been discussing in the conditions of toilers in different parts of the globe is underlined by the fact that the imperialist countries, with 14 percent of the world's population, consume nearly 60 percent of the electricity; the United States alone, with 5 percent of the world's population, consumes more than a quarter of the electricity.

Sub-Saharan Africa, on the other hand, accounts for 9 percent of the world's population but uses 1 percent of global electricity output. In the Ivory Coast, one of the more economically developed countries of West Africa, 13 percent of the rural population has electricity. (And don't forget, we're just dealing here with *access* to electricity, not its reliability or affordability; those are additional questions.) In Ghana, 4 percent of the rural population has access to electricity. In South Africa the figure is now more than 27 percent of the population. Much of that has been achieved in the past half decade alone, inasmuch as the former apartheid regime gave priority to electricity only in areas populated by whites.

In Asia, more than 20 percent of the rural population in Thailand still has no access to electrification of any kind; in Pakistan more than 40 percent; and in Nepal more than 90 percent.

WHAT ABOUT THE SITUATION in Latin America and the Caribbean four decades after the John F. Kennedy administration's "Alliance for Progress"? In Argentina, one of the most industrially developed countries anywhere in the semicolonial world, 10 percent of the population lives without electricity, and several times that percentage in rural areas, where nearly 2.5 million people have no modern power sources. In Brazil, another of the most industrialized Third World countries, nearly 40 percent of rural areas are still not electrified, and some 10 percent of urban areas as well. Two-thirds of rural toilers have no access to electricity in Nicaragua; more than 30 percent in Jamaica; and more than a quarter in Ecuador.

What about Panama, the country that has "benefited" from a century of "treaties" giving U.S. imperialism control over a strategic slice of its territory, and from the American dollar, and from the Pentagon's bases in the Canal Zone? What about that land, which Washington invaded just a little more than a decade ago, killing or maiming thousands with its firebombs and shelling? More than half of Panama's rural population has no access to electricity, nor do more than a quarter of those who live in the cities.

Cuba stands out. With 95 percent of the population having access to electricity, the government is now organizing to complete the job. It has undertaken the installation of solar panels to ensure that even in the most remote mountainous areas of the island there is electricity for the schools and light so people can read, discuss, watch television, and organize cultural activity at night. So that town and country can move toward an equivalence of time available for productive social activity by the toilers. They are able to do this because, as in Soviet Russia in Lenin's time, an alliance of the workers and peasants remains the foundation of the revolution.

World figures on electrification are a gauge of the vast disparities in social and cultural development today brought about by capitalist social relations, and the tendency of those disparities to increase. The imperialist rulers have no intention of shaving their profits or forgiving any debts in order to bring electricity to the toilers of the semicolonial world. They could care less about destroying health, safety, or the natural environment in those countries. The industrially advanced capitalist powers are increasingly seeking to use areas of Africa, Asia, and Latin America as disposal sites for hazardous wastes of all kinds.

Today, coal is the most widely used energy source in the world. This is especially marked in Asia, where coal accounts for more than 60 percent of power generation, and Africa, where it supplies more than 70 percent. (South America is an exception, where hydropower is the primary energy source and relatively little coal is used. Oil and natural gas are the main power sources in the Middle East.)

Coal-fired power, as most of us know from direct experience, takes a substantial toll on public health and the natural environment. In the United States, for example, where just over half the electricity is produced by burning coal, the resulting pollutants are estimated to cause some fifteen thousand premature deaths each year. And the consequences are worse in much of the rest of the world, where costly "clean-coal" technologies are both less available and less used. Smokestack "scrubbers," which the U.S. coal operators and utilities bosses resist in their drive for profits, can substantially reduce a number of harmful by-products, but not carbon dioxide and other gases that affect the earth's atmosphere. And coal burning is responsible for more than 70 percent of carbon dioxide emissions from electrical production worldwide, and more than a third of such emissions from energy output of all kinds.

In *America's Road to Socialism*, a half a century ago Jim Cannon pointed to another advantage of finding alternatives to coal-fired power that we continue to take seriously today. "We can visualize a great system of power stations generated by atomic energy," he says, "taking the burden of labor from the shoulders of half a million coal miners. . . ."[16] That remains our goal: to free miners from mining. If profit maximization were not the guiding principle of mine management, of course, much could be done right now to reduce the risks from methane explosions, collapsed roofs, coal dust, and other dangers. But why subject workers to the dangers inherent in underground mining if it's not socially necessary to do so?

THE EARTH STILL HAS LOTS of coal, and it will undoubtedly remain a power source for years to come. But it's not the solution to meeting humanity's long-term energy needs. Nor, for the foreseeable future, are solar power, wind power, or other renewable energy sources. These sources *can* meet certain select needs, as the Cuban government is showing today. But producing and deploying solar panels and windmills on a scale sufficient to reliably light the world and keep factories running would itself use up enormous quantities of energy and natural resources, as well as acreage in the case of wind power. Not to mention the production of toxic industrial wastes in the process.

In contrast to the industrialized powers of the imperialist world, the 79 percent of humanity who live in the semicolonial countries have little or no access to nuclear power, which produces the greatest amount of energy with the least use of resources and the smallest output of atmospheric pollution. In France, for example, nearly 80 percent of electricity is now produced by nuclear power, and the figure approaches one-quarter in the imperialist countries as a whole. While the figure is still a bit under

16. James P. Cannon, *America's Road to Socialism* (New York: Pathfinder, 1953, 1975), p. 93 [2012 printing].

20 percent in the United States, the more than 100 reactors here produce the largest absolute amount of nuclear power of any country in the world. In South Asia, on the other hand, the figure is only 2 percent, and just 6 percent in East Asia. It's less than 1 percent in Latin America and the Caribbean, and zero for all practical purposes in the Middle East and Africa.[17]

SINCE THE MID-1970S, the Socialist Workers Party has opposed the production and use of nuclear power in the United States. We've held this position because the owners of capital and their government are incapable, by the laws that drive their system, of placing human beings above profits in addressing the questions posed by the operation of nuclear power plants: the design and operation of nuclear reactor cores to prevent meltdowns,

---

17. According to the World Nuclear Association, as of 2004 there were 437 operating nuclear power reactors worldwide, as well as 30 under construction and 32 on order or planned. Of those under construction, half are in semicolonial countries in Asia, largely India (30 percent), China (7 percent), and south Korea (3 percent); a fifth are in Russia; and one-tenth are elsewhere in Eastern or Central Europe. Of those on order or planned, 27 percent are in south Korea, 13 percent, in China, and 6 percent in Latin America (Argentina and Brazil). Aside from Finland, where one new nuclear power plant is planned, Japan is the only imperialist country with reactors on order or planned (40 percent of the world total). Following the 1979 accident at the Three Mile Island reactor in Pennsylvania, no new orders for nuclear power plants have been made in the United States; much the same is true for Western Europe. Nuclear power's share in total world electricity output, however, more than doubled from 8 percent in 1979 to above 16 percent in 1987, remaining at roughly that level ever since.

the manufacture and redundancy of secure containment vessels, and the disposal of radioactive and other toxic waste products.

But our position is political; it isn't based on the half-life of an atom. Marxists start from the historically demonstrated capacity of human beings to transform nature, raise the productivity of social labor, and advance the accessibility of civilization and culture to more and more of the world's toilers.

That's the main thing that's wrong with Fred Halstead's argument in *What Working People Should Know about the Dangers of Nuclear Power,* a pamphlet we've used as part of our propaganda arsenal for more than twenty years.[18] From the pamphlet's very first sentence—"Nuclear power's special danger to health, safety, and even life itself can be summed up in one word: *radiation*"—to its very last—"[W]e can end nuclear power's threat to the very existence of the human race"—it approaches the safety issues posed by nuclear energy and radioactive wastes as immutable facts of nature, not as social and political questions that can be addressed and solved by the toilers. It does not start with where the development of nuclear power—and the questions of safety, health, and environmental degradation posed not only by it but also by alternative energy sources—fits along the line of march of workers and farmers toward the revolutionary struggle for national liberation and socialism on a world scale. It is in large part a valuable layman's explanation— atomic diagrams and all—of the ABCs of nuclear physics: what's an atom? what causes radiation? what's the difference between fission and fusion? how do reactors work? and so on.

---

18. Fred Halstead, *What Working People Should Know about the Dangers of Nuclear Power* (New York: Pathfinder, 1981).

The point is not that much of the basic information in the pamphlet is necessarily wrong (although the virtual dismissal of the damaging health and environmental consequences of coal combustion, including the production of carbon dioxide waste, is certainly mistaken). But the pamphlet avoids the central *political questions* the revolutionary workers movement needs to address. Nuclear power will continue to be developed. The question is what class will end up guiding this process and in whose interests.

The competition of capitals, the drive to maximize profits, spurs technological innovation under capitalism and will continue to do so for as long as this social system exists. At the same time, these same laws of capital accumulation press the employing class to subordinate (and often suppress) scientific and technological developments that would benefit competitors—and the producers—in order to maximize profits. In the process, capitalists display wanton disregard for the health and safety of workers and the broader population. Nor do they care one whit about the long-term or short-term consequences for the natural environment.

A testimony to the barbaric, antihuman character of capitalism is the reality that many of the greatest advances in science and technology, including nuclear power, are by-products of the rulers' preparations for war and mass slaughter. That's been the case throughout the history of class society, in fact, but the consequences in the imperialist epoch genuinely threaten the existence of humanity.

It's useful to recall that the Socialist Workers Party supported the Cuban government's decision in the early 1980s to enter into an agreement with the Soviet Union for financial and technical assistance in building a nuclear power plant at Juraguá. Our position on nuclear power in the United States has never been an ahistorical, universal nostrum. The Cuban government was seeking to lessen the country's energy dependence on oil imports from the Soviet Union, Mexico, Venezuela, or anywhere else. Both the U.S. government and Cuban-American counterrevolutionaries cynically tried to win sympathy for their campaign against the Cuban Revolution by seeking to whip up hysteria in Florida about the reactor and to draw in middle-class forces from environmental and antinuclear power groups in the United States.

The Cuban government was forced to suspend construction on the reactor in 1992, when the collapse of the Stalinist regime in the Soviet Union brought an abrupt halt to needed financial and technical assistance. After nearly a decade of hard negotiations with the Russian government, the Cubans concluded they would not be able to obtain terms that were either affordable or offered sufficient guarantees they could operate and maintain the plant, so they announced in December 2000 that they no longer planned to resume work on the project. But if the government in Cuba saw the possibility and need to restart a nuclear power program, we would approach the issues posed from the same political perspective as we did the Juraguá reactor: that of the international proletariat.

WE TAKE THIS POSITION not because Cuba made a socialist revolution four decades ago, not because it is a workers state, not because it continues to be guided by a revolutionary leadership. We do so because Cuba is a country that remains semicolonial in its economic development. The communist movement equally defends steps that may be taken to expand and extend electrification by governments in India, Iran, Brazil, South Africa, or

Photos: Landov

"Scarcity has nothing to do with why more than a third of humanity has no access to electricity, goes to bed hungry, or has no access to potable water. Those are social questions, class questions, political questions."

TOP: Women in Sri Lanka fetch water, 2004. Throughout semicolonial world, lack of electrical pumps means hundreds of millions are forced to carry water by hand, a task that largely falls on women.
BOTTOM: Uranium enrichment plant in Resende, Brazil, 2004, which imperialist representatives, under UN auspices, insisted on "inspecting," in violation of Brazilian sovereignty. Nearly 40 percent of rural Brazil lacks electricity. Nuclear-powered generation is only possible road to development for many of world's toilers.

elsewhere in the semicolonial world. The Cuban government and Communist Party, too, would reject any singling out of Cuba in this regard.

Given the unmet energy needs of billions across the globe, especially in semicolonial countries; the rising extraction and refining costs of the world's oil resources; and accumulating and accelerating damage to the earth's atmosphere from the burning of oil, coal, and other fossil fuels, nuclear reactors *will* be used to generate a growing percentage of the world's electrical power in the twenty-first century. That's for sure, and necessarily so. The question is how long will the design and construction of containment vessels, the monitoring of reactor operations, and disposal of atomic waste products—with all the consequences for public health and safety—be carried out by governments beholden to the imperialist ruling families and other capitalist exploiters. How long before these vital matters, including the eventual transition away from nuclear power toward other, safer energy sources yet to be developed, will be organized by workers and farmers governments acting in the interests of the great majority of humanity. The stakes in the resolution of that question—an outcome that will be settled in historic class battles—could not be clearer.

The dangers of nuclear power are not an argument against its potential benefits in advancing electrification of the world, but an argument *for* organizing the toilers to take power from the hands of the capitalist exploiters. The communist movement does not have "a position on nuclear power," for or against. We have a proletarian internationalist course to advance the revolutionary struggle for national liberation and socialism. Along that road, vanguard workers in the imperialist countries make clear to the people of the semicolonial world that we reject the politics of our own ruling classes and support the extension of electrification to the billions around the earth who are forced to live and toil without it. We will fight to win the workers, farmers, and middle-class layers we can influence to understand and support this course as well.

Free trade: 'workers go to the wall either way'

Our politics, proletarian politics, on what the capitalist rulers call "free trade" also start with the world.

In his January 1848 "Speech on the Question of Free Trade," Karl Marx warned working people and democrats not to be "deluded by the abstract word Freedom!" Whose freedom? he asked. "Not the freedom of one individual in relation to another, but freedom of Capital to crush the worker." Under capitalist social relations, Marx pointed out, whether free trade or protection happens to be current government policy, either way the worker "goes to the wall."[19] Since Marx first prepared that speech for publication more than a century and a half ago, the structure of world capitalism has changed significantly, with the rise and consolidation of the global imperialist order. What hasn't changed, however, is the correctness of Marx's concluding words: that in judging the trade policies of one or another capitalist government, the position of the workers movement is determined by what "hastens the Social Revolution."

We start with the interests of the working class, which is an international class. We have no blueprint good for all times, all situations, and all places. With regard to products coming into the United States, our position on free trade is very simple: *we're for it*. Communists in

19. Karl Marx, "Speech on the Question of Free Trade," *MECW*, vol. 6, pp. 463–65.

other imperialist countries take the same position with respect to "their own" governments. We're unconditionally opposed to the rulers of the United States imposing protectionist barriers of any kind under any pretext on imported goods. And we're opposed to Washington imposing an embargo on the export of goods to Cuba, Iraq, north Korea, Iran—or any imperialist country either, for that matter!

We do everything possible to expose the "free trade" demagogy of finance capital. The rulers' trade policy, from start to finish, is a *national policy*. It aims to advance the national interests of the exploiting class, including balancing the conflicting profit needs of capitalist sectors that are vulnerable to competition on the world market to quite different degrees. Under the banner of free trade, the U.S. government uses so-called antidumping clauses, "environmental" and "labor standards" restrictions, "human rights" demagogy, and other measures to carry out brutal and aggressive trade wars not only against its imperialist rivals but with special ferocity against the semicolonial countries. By the World Bank's own conservative figures, for example, trade barriers by the industrially advanced countries cost what the bank labels the world's fifty least-developed countries some $2.5 billion in export income annually. Almost half of that is accounted for by U.S. barriers alone—and a high percentage of that is basic agricultural products.

All the talk from the White House, Congress, and in the big-business press about the "complexities" and breakdowns of international negotiations to advance "free trade" is a self-serving smoke screen. The U.S. rulers need do only one thing: declare that all goods coming into the United States are free of tariffs and nontariff barriers of any kind. That's what the Socialist Workers Party demands in the United States, and what our comrades demand of the governments in Canada, France, Sweden, Iceland, Australia, New Zealand, and the United Kingdom.

That is not what communists demand in most countries in the world today, however. The workings of the world capitalist market bring about an enormous, an unconscionable, transfer to the imperialist countries of the wealth produced by the workers and peasants of Africa, the Middle East, Latin America, and most of Asia and the Pacific. That extortion is guaranteed not primarily by "unfair" terms of trade imposed from the outside on the world market. It is guaranteed above all by the differential value of labor power and the gap in productivity of labor between the imperialist countries on the one hand, and those oppressed and exploited by imperialism on the other—a differential that not only underlies unequal exchange but relentlessly reproduces and increases it.

Imperialism warps the economic structures of the semicolonial world. The "comparative advantage" of oppressed nations in the world capitalist market is largely restricted to producing and exporting agricultural produce and raw materials, as well as in recent decades serving as an "export platform" for light manufactures or other industrial goods often made in imperialist-owned factories. Even with regard to these goods, countries in the semicolonial world get slapped down any time they try to horn in on markets sought by the titans of agriculture and industry in North America, Europe, or Japan.

Meanwhile, big business in the United States and in the other imperialist powers exports heavy industrial goods, technology, machine tools, other manufactures, and agricultural produce—and large amounts of capital as well. Today the capital exported to semicolonial countries in particular takes the form not only of buying

up agricultural land, factories, retail and wholesale businesses, insurance companies, banks, and mineral rights.
It also takes the form of loans that ensnare these countries in a vortex of debt slavery to imperialist banks and
governments, often through the intermediary of "international" financial institutions such as the World Bank
and International Monetary Fund.

THE CURRENCIES OF a growing number of countries in
Latin America and other semicolonial countries have
recently been tied even more directly to the dollar. Both
Ecuador and El Salvador have actually adopted the U.S.
dollar as the national currency over the past year, joining
Panama, which has been shackled to the greenback since
the closing years of World War II. But the most striking
example is Argentina. That was U.S. imperialism's "free
market" showcase for the Third World in the early 1990s.
The secret to its "inflation-free growth" was said to be the
Argentine bourgeoisie's decision a decade ago to peg the
peso one-to-one to the dollar. Since the mid-1990s, however, the overvalued peso has exacerbated a deepening
recession, unemployment has soared, even the caloric
intake of working people in countryside and city has
dropped. And worse is yet to come. There has also been
a response: repeated social explosions first in this city or
province, next in that one, then in another.[20]

---

20. The Argentine crisis reached a new stage in December 2001.
Despite years of government and employer assaults on jobs, wages,
and social benefits, the regime defaulted on $100 billion of gov-
ernment bonds, owned largely by capitalists in Western Europe.
The peso was cut loose from the dollar, and its value plummeted
by 75 percent, with devastating consequences for working people

In Mexico, U.S. finance capital has pressured the government to open up the banking system to direct imperialist penetration and growing domination. With government barriers to foreign ownership of Mexican banks now lifted, Citibank earlier this year purchased Banamex, the second-largest banking group in the country. That means more imperialist capital will pour into the country,[21] increasing the already staggering foreign debt and further pressuring living and working conditions. A similar process is beginning to unfold in south Korea, with the takeover of Daewoo by General Motors and more imperialist buyouts on the way. Nowadays few are talking about "Asian Tigers."

Under the administrations of both Presidents William Clinton and George W. Bush, Washington has been pushing to impose what it calls the Free Trade Area of

---

and broad layers of the middle class. Widespread strikes, demonstrations, and factory occupations forced the resignation of four presidents in a row between December 2001 and January 2002. Over the next year, as economic growth fell by 12 percent, joblessness shot up to nearly 25 percent and inflation reached 40 percent. By mid-2004, government jobless figures were still almost 15 percent and nearly half of Argentines were living below the official poverty line, while international finance capital continued to stand behind wealthy bondholders in rejecting the Argentine government's offer to pay off the defaulted debt at $0.25 on the dollar.

21. Nearly 80 percent of commercial bank assets in Mexico are today owned by banks in the United States, Western Europe, Canada, or Japan—including all five of the country's largest banks. This is up from around 1 percent a decade ago, when the imperialist powers forced open the gates during the 1994–95 "peso crisis" in Mexico. See "So Far from God, So Close to Orange County," in Jack Barnes, *Capitalism's World Disorder: Working-Class Politics at the Millennium* (New York: Pathfinder, 1999), pp. 55–63 [2012 printing].

the Americas (FTAA), a metastasization of the North American Free Trade Agreement (NAFTA), on the rest of Latin America and the Caribbean.[22] This new Yankee "Good Neighbor" policy for the twenty-first century will open up the countries and peoples of the Western Hemisphere to even greater penetration and predation by U.S. capital and commodities. Terms of trade will become more unequal, not less.

In response, Cuban president Fidel Castro has proposed to working-class parties, popular organizations, and trade unions throughout the region that they demand a nationwide vote in every country of South America, Central America, and the Caribbean on ratification of this imperialist-instigated agreement. Let the people vote on the FTAA! We support that demand and through our press, our election campaigns, and our weekly forums explain why. Even as we simultaneously explain to our compañeros in Cuba and elsewhere throughout the Americas why in the United States the campaign against the FTAA waged by trade union officials and assorted liberal and radical groupings has a completely different content—a reactionary, chauvinist, pro-imperialist one that we expose and oppose in every way possible.

'Overpopulation' myth

Communists in the United States will be able to develop our politics and strategy, set our tasks and priorities, and build a revolutionary proletarian party only if we are simultaneously working as part of a world movement of

---

22. For a discussion of NAFTA, see section III, "Historic Shift in World Capital Flows," in the 1994 talk by Jack Barnes, "Imperialism's March toward Fascism and War," published in *New International* no. 10 (1994), pp. 296–322 [2011 printing].

political equals. This proletarian internationalist perspective is the opposite of the nationalist viewpoint promoted by the U.S. bourgeoisie and aped to one degree or another by virtually every petty-bourgeois current in the working-class movement.

The American nationalism we reject takes a particularly virulent form in the chauvinist demagogy of ultrarightist forces such as those of Patrick Buchanan. One of the axes of Buchanan's politics is sounding an alarm that the population is exploding among the already majority black-, brown-, and yellow-skinned peoples of the world while fertility rates among those with white skin in Europe and North America are plunging. Combined with growing immigration to the industrialized countries, Buchanan says, these demographic trends spell the doom of what he calls "Western culture and civilization," and what many of his supporters bluntly call "white (Christian) America," or sometimes, in a more mixed crowd, just "the West."

Ever since Parson Thomas Malthus in 1798 published his tract on the dangers of "overpopulation," the Right and Left alike in bourgeois politics, using slightly different rhetoric, have promoted periodic panics on this theme. Over the past half century, liberals have been the most vigorous Cassandras warning of the "population bomb."

The racist thrust of all such campaigns today lies right on the surface: the idea is that the dusky races, not only from sub-Saharan Africa but also from Asia and the Americas, are not fully human—or at least not yet fully civilized. But the capitalist ruling classes and their servants among the professional layers face an irresolvable dilemma in addressing the intertwined questions of world population and immigration. The propertied classes desperately need more and more of "them" to

continue reconstituting the reserve army of the unemployed and—the rulers hope—hold down wage rates and
demands for better working and living conditions that
cut deeply into their extraction of surplus value. But the
bourgeoisie, and especially the petty bourgeoisie, also
fear being swallowed in a sea of "them." Moreover, we
are now warned by the rulers and their propagandists,
in increasingly strident tones, that the accelerating mi-
gration from North Africa, the Middle East, and South
Asia is planting "terrorists" in our midst.

MALCOLM X WENT straight for this raw nerve nearly
forty years ago when he mocked the hysteria in bourgeois
public opinion over the prospect of the People's Republic of China developing nuclear weapons. "Thank God,
they don't have delivery systems" was the American rulers'
only consolation. So Malcolm rubbed it in. Once they get
the bomb, the Chinese won't need to worry about delivery systems, he chided. There are so many Chinese they
can "hand carry" it!

Fear of this population/immigration explosion sce-
nario is deep in the class psychology of the bourgeoisie
and better-off petty- bourgeois layers. It often goes hand
in hand with demands to crack down on immigrants—
not with the aim of cutting off the needed flow of cheap
labor to exploit, but of creating an atmosphere of intimi-
dation and looming deportations that can "keep them in
their place." Overpopulation hype is always accompanied
by barely repressed anxieties rooted in the feared loss of
ill-gotten gains. It's always accompanied by worries about
the "high crime rates" that can reach into "my own back-
yard" as the "underclass" increases. Bourgeois "common
sense" emphasizes the "limits of growth," "unsustainable

pressures" on the environment and biosphere, "exhaustion" of natural resources, drying up of the staff of life—in a phrase, *ecological Armageddon.* In a word, chicken-littleism. These are the socially acceptable euphemisms used to camouflage the deepest terrors of privileged liberals. That class bias is stronger by far than their "liberalism."

This political consequence of accelerated social inequality and class privilege is the central point of *The Bell Curve: Intelligence and Class Structure in American Life* by Richard J. Herrnstein and Charles Murray.[23] As the authors put it in the second-to-last chapter, a "professor's best-selling book may be a diatribe against the punitive criminal justice system, but that doesn't mean that he doesn't vote with his feet to move to a safe neighborhood." Commenting on the term "secession of the successful" coined by Robert Reich, secretary of labor in the first Clinton administration, Herrnstein and Murray continue: "The current symbol of this phenomenon is the gated community, secure behind its walls and guard posts. . . . Or the proliferation of private security forces for companies, apartment houses, schools, malls, and anywhere else where people with money want to be safe."[24]

----

23. See "The 'Bell Curve': The scandal of class privilege" from "So Far from God, So Close to Orange County," in Barnes, *Capitalism's World Disorder*, pp. 181–93 [2012 printing].

24. Richard J. Herrnstein and Charles Murray, *The Bell Curve: Intelligence and Class Structure in American Life* (New York: Free Press, 1994), pp. 515, 517. A Census Bureau study in 2001 reported that about 6 percent of households in the United States—some 7 million—are now in developments behind walls or fences. A 2003 book on the subject adds that one-third of all new communities in southern California are gated and that 80 percent of homes worth more than $300,000 in Tampa, Florida, are within gates. The number of people employed by private security companies

Buchanan's own nightmare scenarios, of course, are based in part on projections of current population trends. Just since 1950, the percentage of the world's population living in the imperialist countries has declined from 22 percent to 14 percent. And some studies project that the "white" population of Europe will decline by as much as 25 percent over the next half century. Not as bad as the Black Plague of 1348, which reduced the population of Europe by one-third to one-half. But that's cold comfort for the likes of Buchanan and his European co-thinkers!

The assertion that population growth is exploding geometrically everywhere else in the world is not true, of course. In fact, it is actually decelerating, leveling off. The "baby bomb" propagandists ignore the reality that birth rates decline as toilers emigrate from countryside to city, as women gain access to education and enter the urban workforce, as living standards rise, and as access to modern contraception expands.

Two OF THE WEALTHIEST and most prominent of the nouveaux riches in America, Microsoft's Bill Gates and Berkshire Hathaway's Warren Buffet, are both among the world's largest individual contributors to population control programs for the semicolonial countries. And CNN's Ted Turner recently donated $1 billion to support United Nations programs to stop the world's peoples, as he earlier put it, from "breeding like a plague of locusts." But their combined charitable efforts are dwarfed by the unstoppable social consequences of the workings of capital itself, which continue to expel millions of rural debt

---

in the United States nearly doubled to 1.9 million between 1980 and 2000, according to the Security Industry Association.

slaves from the land and drive them into towns and cities. In urban areas a new blessed event is no longer another pair of hands soon to work in the fields, but a new mouth to feed in face of family members' desperate search to sell their labor power and gain a living wage.

Women pressed by necessity into the urban job market can no longer tend their children as they did even when families worked in the fields. And extended units of grandparents, uncles, aunts, cousins, and siblings break down in the cities. As capital to varying degrees enlarges the middle classes throughout the semicolonial world, women who gain jobs, more education, a greater degree of equality and independence, and better conditions give birth to fewer children on average as well.

What's more, since the early 1990s the social devastation that has accompanied all varieties of capitalist "shock therapy" across the workers states of the former Soviet Union and Eastern Europe—as the imperialists have pressed the newly dominant sections of the governing castes to unleash the sway of the law of value in production, commerce, and finance—has both dramatically shortened life expectancies and also led to a sharp decline in birth rates in many of these countries.

So, it's simply not true that there is some steady rise in fertility rates outside the imperialist countries, irrespective of shifts in class structure, urban migrations, and other deep-going social transformations. In fact, the trend is the opposite. Nine of the fifteen largest semicolonial countries today have birth rates lower than that of the United States in 1965.

Take Mexico, for example. Being right next door and the largest single origin of immigration to the United States, it is a particular source of alarm for both Buchanan and liberal doomsayers alike. The fact is that the birth rate in Mexico has dropped from nearly seven children per woman in the late 1960s to under two-and-a-half children on average today. That is an enormous demographic shift in the short span of forty years.

Or take India, the country with the second-largest population in the world. The fertility rate there has fallen to an average of three children per woman from around six in 1950.[25]

No abstract laws of population

None of the current overpopulation disciples add anything fundamental to Malthus's reactionary arguments, which were answered most succinctly by Karl Marx in *Capital* some 135 years ago.[26]

First, Marx punctured the fallacy at the foundation of Malthus's position, that is, that population growth will inevitably outstrip the productivity of agricultural labor and lead to catastrophic food shortages and famine. To the contrary, Marx responded, the earth "continuously improves, as long as it is treated correctly," thus the production of food can expand much more quickly than population.[27] Marx's assessment has been confirmed

---

25. According to United Nations figures, the birth rate for semi-colonial countries in Asia, Africa, and Latin America has declined from an average of 5.4 per woman in the 1970–75 period to an estimated 2.9 in the first half decade of the twenty-first century—a 46.2 percent decline in thirty-five years.

26. A good selection of writings by Karl Marx and Frederick Engels, no longer in print, is: Ronald L. Meek, ed., *Marx and Engels on Malthus* (New York: International Publishers, 1954). It was later reissued under the title *Marx and Engels on the Population Bomb* (Berkeley: Ramparts, 1971).

27. Karl Marx, *Capital*, vol. 3 (London: Penguin, 1981), p. 916.

many times over. Just since 1960, total grain production worldwide increased at a rate 25 percent above that of population growth over that same period. As Marx also explained, however, the capitalist market system deepens class inequalities and ensures the spread of malnutrition, hunger, and outright starvation amid plenty—the plight of more than 2 billion people today, according to United Nations figures. That's twice the population of the entire world in Malthus's time.

SECOND, MARX EXPLAINED that "every particular historical mode of production has its own special laws of population, which are historically valid within that particular sphere. An abstract law of population exists only for plants and animals, and even then only in the absence of any historical intervention by man." Under capitalism, Marx said, what appears to be overpopulation is in fact "a disposable industrial reserve army" that helps the capitalist class keep wage rates low and is "always ready for exploitation by capital in the interests of capital's own changing" profit needs. "The working population therefore produces both the accumulation of capital and the means by which it is itself made relatively superfluous," he wrote, "and it does this to an extent which is always increasing. This is the law of population peculiar to the capitalist mode of production. . . ."[28]

In the imperialist epoch, this reserve army of labor increasingly takes on worldwide dimensions, as workers driven off the land, fleeing wretched slums across Asia, Africa, and Latin America, migrate across borders in hopes of finding a living wage in the industrialized capitalist

28. Marx, *Capital*, vol. 1 (London: Penguin, 1986), p. 784.

countries of North America, Europe, Australia, New Zealand, and even to an increasing degree today—Japan.

The Malthusian hype about the world running out of food goes hand in hand with projections that other resources are being exhausted by "population pressure" as well. These predictions are always accompanied by rationalizations as to why workers and farmers around the world must tighten our belts in the interests of "future generations"—in practice, in the interests of the *current generations* of a handful of propertied ruling families and the privileged upper middle classes. A well-known proponent of these views once put it this way: "Giving society cheap, abundant energy would be the equivalent of giving an idiot child a machine gun." The quotation is from Paul Ehrlich, who wrote a best-selling book in 1968 entitled *The Population Bomb*. A few years later Ehrlich, who is a liberal, wrote another book arguing that the world was being stalked by a growing scarcity of key natural resources.

In 1980 a conservative economist named Julian Simon challenged Ehrlich to a bet. If Ehrlich were right about mounting scarcity, then the prices of these commodities would rise over time, as demand outstripped supply. So Simon proposed to Ehrlich: I'll buy $200 worth of each of five metals: tin, tungsten, copper, nickel, and chrome. If the combined price of these five metals was higher ten years later, then Simon would pay Ehrlich the difference. If it was lower Ehrlich would pay Simon. By 1990 the prices of all five metals had dropped, and Ehrlich sent Simon a check for $576.

The wager would have been a no-brainer for Marxists—or anyone else, for that matter, who bothered to take an objective look at the 250-year-long history of industrial capitalism. The fact is that despite various short-

and medium-term trends, the prices of all such resources have gone down historically under capitalism and will continue to do so.

Scarcity has nothing whatsoever to do with why more than a third of humanity has no access to electricity today, or goes to bed without enough food, or has no access to potable water. Those are *social* questions, *class* questions, *political* questions: questions of capitalist income distribution and its continual reproduction.

And these questions are of great importance to communists who live and fight today in a world in which the ranks of the working class continue to swell worldwide in both absolute and relative terms, as well as in social and political weight. They are of great importance in a world in which the worker-peasant alliance becomes not only a more pressing necessity with each passing decade, but objectively more realizable. They are of great importance in a world in which the very workings of capitalism are pulling tens of millions of toilers across oceans, continents, and borders into the United States and other imperialist countries.

What a workers and farmers government will do

Each of us has probably had the experience of reading something twice, three times, or even more and suddenly noticing something we had never read quite the same way before. A phrase jumps out at us because of some experience we've had in the class struggle or some political question we're working through. Recently, in rereading the Constitution of the Socialist Workers Party, I was struck by Article II, the second paragraph: "The purpose of the party shall be to educate and organize the working class in order to establish a workers and farmers government, which will abolish capitalism in the United States *and join in the worldwide struggle for socialism."*

The statement of purpose opens with the revolutionary effort to organize the working class and our allies to establish a government of workers and farmers here—in the United States. That's first and foremost a practical problem and an "American" one. Because this is the state, this is the armed power the mass vanguard of the working class must be led to take on and defeat. We must make a revolution within these boundaries, within the fifty states where the dollar is the currency that, for better or worse, rules supreme.

As the second part of our statement of purpose makes clear, however, we have no illusion that when the workers and farmers of the United States conquer power, socialism can be built in *this* one country any more than in any other one country. Or that such a liberating power can defend itself from antagonists abroad simply by hunkering down and "building socialism." What will have changed is that the working people of the United States will be able to join in the worldwide struggle for socialism with a new and powerful instrument—the single most powerful instrument the toilers can wield, a workers and farmers government. That revolutionary government will be not only the antechamber to the dictatorship of the proletariat in this country, but to an entirely new stage in the *world* revolution as well. Or else it will be overthrown and horrible reaction imposed on the toilers.

I've read Article II of the party constitution before. But it wasn't until I reread it again recently that I was struck by how well it helps us understand the starting point of proletarian internationalism for communists in the United States: conquering power, taking it from the murderous imperialist rulers of this country, is the single biggest contribution that U.S. workers and farmers can and will

"An alliance of workers and farmers is not only a more and more pressing necessity in today's world, it is objectively more realizable."

Farmers throughout capitalist world are squeezed between high-cost inputs and low prices for their produce. **TOP**: Protest by farmers in Ontario, Canada, demands cash relief and government assistance, January 2001. **BOTTOM**: Farmers and workers from the U.S. exchange experiences with Cuban farmers at credit and service cooperative in 2000.

Karl Butts

make to the worldwide fight for socialism. Despite all the organization, discipline, muscle, bone, and blood it will take to accomplish that goal, however, the victory of the socialist revolution in this country will then pose a new set of political tasks that are even more challenging, more essential, and more rewarding in advancing the forward march of humanity.

The establishment of the dictatorship of the proletariat won't bring socialism. It will create the conditions in which the working class can begin to take ever-greater strides toward workers control of industry together with the opening steps toward the management of industry and economic planning. In which farmers, no longer threatened by foreclosure on the land they till, can begin, with the help of toilers in the cities, to revolutionize agricultural production in the interests of humanity today and tomorrow (and can teach the urban population a thing or two, enriching our lives and broadening our culture). In which Blacks can organize under the aegis of the new state power to take rapid, giant strides toward ridding social relations of every vestige of racist prejudice and discrimination. In which women, together with powerful allies, can organize themselves to advance the struggle for their complete emancipation from the oppressive legacy of millennia of class society. And in which the entire weight of the new workers and farmers republic in the United States will be brought to bear to advance every struggle for national liberation and for socialism taking place anywhere in the world.

That's the perspective, that's the world program to which we recruit workers, farmers, and youth in this country. They join the Young Socialists and Socialist Workers Party not only because they are attracted to the perspective of a revolution that promises to put the rapid and thorough elimination of these deeply rooted forms of oppression on the agenda, but because they want to be part of the struggles, on a world scale, out of which something worthy of the name socialism will emerge.

Changing patterns of resistance

For eighty-five years the population of Nebraska declined every decade. The joke was that Nebraska's main export was people. Then in the mid-1990s, all of a sudden the figures reversed. Today, one out of every ten children in Nebraska has parents from Mexico or Central America.

Comrades in California a few days ago went to visit some forty or so workers in the Salinas Valley—everyone there was originally not just from Mexico but from the state of Oaxaca in Mexico. We had made contact with them through another worker from Oaxaca who on a regular basis joins in activities with comrades in the party's Atlanta branch. As it turned out, a good number of these workers had come to the meeting in hopes we could do something to help them solve various immigration problems. Comrades told the workers that on that score, they'd be better off talking to people who know the ropes about immigration law and procedures. We said we are workers and communists who had come to have a political discussion, at the suggestion of several of them we'd worked with before and their friend in Georgia.

Some folks shook hands and left. But about twenty workers stayed, so we began a discussion. Comrades had come prepared to do translation both ways between Spanish and English. But one of the organizers of the meeting politely asked our translators to slow down, since everything had to be translated *twice*: from English into Spanish, and after that from Spanish into two different Indian languages, and back around the barn again to English.

It's a story that underlines a political point we're learning and relearning in many of the garment shops and packinghouses where we have jobs, and in strike solidarity work and other social struggles we're involved in: while learning Spanish is important for worker-bolsheviks (we're doing it a little more consistently once again, as well as helping workers we recruit who are not comfortable in English learn it), working people engaged as equals in a fight can and do find ways to communicate with each other.

The party is becoming more integrated into the working class as it exists, and into the working-class resistance that is transforming the possibilities to build a proletarian party. For example, we're in the midst of the fight being organized today by immigrants' rights groups in several states demanding repeal of the requirement that Social Security numbers be included on drivers licenses. We're virtually the only ones explaining the stakes for all workers, for the entire U.S. labor movement, and calling on the unions to throw their weight into this fight. These new state laws—which make it more difficult for undocumented workers to get drivers licenses and hold a job, and increase their vulnerability to harassment and deportation—are at the same time another step toward imposing a national identity card system on the entire population of the United States.

But we have to be clear. The communist movement doesn't have an orientation to immigrant workers. We have an orientation to the vanguard of the working class, the vanguard of the labor movement, the vanguard involved in union, social, and political struggles in defense of the toilers against the employing class, its government, and its political parties. We join in these myriad fights and find as many ways as we can to present and discuss a revolutionary program in the interests of the working class. As we do so, we bump into a lot of immigrant workers. Yet we're sharply aware that the vast majority of workers in this country, including many who are part of the new vanguard that is emerging, are not recent immigrants. Some of our biggest sales of *Militant* subscriptions over the past several months, for example, have been to coal miners in Pennsylvania, Colorado, Wyoming, and New Mexico, workers who are predominantly U.S.-born and whose first language is English. We've had good sales of the *Militant* and other literature to the families of uranium miners in the West fighting for medical coverage and compensation, in face of the devastating consequences of the mining bosses' disregard for workers' health, safety, and lives.

All this is part of a single class reality, as the evidence continues to mount that there has been a sea change in the pattern of resistance by working people, a refusal to simply be pushed back by the employers and their government, a tendency to reach out to others resisting the rulers' assaults. If we follow the existing lines of resistance among working people in city and countryside—and if we act on the logic of politics and are ready to adapt our forms accordingly to maximize our response to the breadth of these opportunities—then our course of action will take us deeper into embryonic social movements of our class and its allies. It will take us deeper into the unions and the struggle to transform them into fighting proletarian organizations that think socially and act politically.

The present as history

An integral part of our response to the sea change in working-class politics has been the lead taken by comrades in the Atlanta and Washington, D.C., branches to deepen our work together with farmers who are Black fighting against foreclosure and against all the forms of racist discrimination they have faced from federal farm agencies and in securing affordable credit. These comrades have also been encouraging us to take seriously the *history* of these current struggles, their place in an ongoing continuity that reaches back to the U.S. Civil War—the Second American Revolution—and above all the decades following that war in the countryside, towns, and cities across the South.

Many of these farmers are fighting to continue cultivating land that their kin have farmed for generations. For a Black family in the U.S. South to have held onto land for that long means that previous generations fought and survived the lynch-mob terror of organized white-supremacist night riders that continued, and often accelerated, in the wake of the defeat of post–Civil War Radical Reconstruction. This came closer to fascist violence on a broad scale, and over an extended period, than anything else ever seen in this country.

In the decade following the defeat of the slavocracy in 1865, the rising Northern industrial bourgeoisie—now reknitting links with powerful landholding, commercial, and emerging manufacturing interests across the South—settled once and for all that it had no intention of meeting the aspirations of freed slaves for a radical land reform to provide them "40 acres and a mule." Doing so, first of all, would deprive these exploiters of a cheap supply of jobless laborers. What's more, the bourgeoisie correctly feared that an alliance of free farmers, Black and white, together with the growing industrial working class in the cities could pose a strong challenge to intensifying exploitation in town and country, South and North.

So in 1877 the U.S. rulers withdrew federal troops

from the states of the old Confederacy. These troops had been the armed force standing between the freed Black toilers, on the one hand, and gangs of reactionary vigilantes, on the other. Throughout the closing decades of the nineteenth century and well into the twentieth, successive generations of organizations such as the Knights of the White Camelia, the Ku Klux Klan, the White Citizens Councils, and many others—named and unnamed—carried out an unrelenting reign of terror against the Black population in the South.

This systematic violence helped the capitalists drive toilers who were Black into virtual peonage as sharecroppers and tenant farmers, and made it possible for Jim Crow segregation to be imposed in one Southern state after another. These gangs were also organized to break the spirit of any class-conscious worker or farmer anywhere in the South who wasn't Black—"nigger lovers"— and to prevent them from linking arms with toilers who were Black in common struggles for land, for public education, for cheap credit and railway rates, for labor union rights, or anything else in the interests of the oppressed and exploited.

Some of you may have already seen the exhibit of lynching photographs that has been in New York this year and will travel to other cities. If not, I recommend it.[29] Many of the photos are actual postcards of these outrages, produced by the organizers of the lynch mobs and widely distributed to popularize and legitimatize lynching as a

29. The exhibit, "Without Sanctuary: Photographs and Postcards of Lynching in America," remained on tour in the United States in mid-2004. Also see James Allen et al, *Without Sanctuary: Lynching Photography in America* (Santa Fe, New Mexico: Twin Palms, 2000).

"family activity"—yes, a family activity—and to try to limit resistance by Blacks throughout the South. They are a powerful reminder of the history we've been discussing here. The accompanying text and other materials point out that the decision to steal land from Black farmers often precipitated the lynchings.

Working alongside farmers who are fighting to stay on the land, we should know this history—our history. The land isn't just a way to make a living. Nor is it just a symbol. The current resistance is often a link in battles that go back more than a century and a quarter. Together with fights by workers and the labor movement, these hard-fought battles by generations of farmers helped hold off some of the most reactionary consequences of the defeat of Radical Reconstruction that would have set back, much further than they did, the struggles of working people in the United States. And they helped make possible a new wave of struggle decades later that by the end of the 1960s had brought the Jim Crow system crashing down.

THE CIVIL RIGHTS BATTLES of the 1950s, '60s, and '70s in rural counties, small towns, and cities across the South, in turn, helped transform the possibilities for workers and farmers alike throughout this country, and throughout other parts of the world under assault by Washington. Among other things, the conquests of this mass proletarian movement laid a foundation for a common struggle with common demands by working farmers in the United States today, as part of a worker-farmer alliance resisting the profit-driven course of the capitalist class. It attracted, politicized, and gave courage to several generations of youth who would provide the energy for struggles against the Vietnam War, for democratic rights, for women's emancipation, and for a political radicalization in this country.

The results of history remain alive, so long as the class questions posed by giant social and political conflicts remain unresolved and the true class lessons become a weapon in the hands of militants today. The full consequences of the defeat of Radical Reconstruction, for example, will only be uprooted following the victory of a workers revolution in this country. That's why struggles over state governments displaying the Confederate battle flag, or over statues or holidays in tribute to political or military leaders of the slaveholders' rebellion, continue to have weight in the class struggle many decades—indeed almost a century and a half—later.

THESE FIGHTS IN South Carolina, Mississippi, and elsewhere are not about Blacks and supporters of civil rights being mean to somebody in the South whose great granddaddy was a Confederate soldier who "fought bravely" and was "a good man."[30] Many Confederate soldiers did fight

---

30. On January 17, 2000, some fifty thousand people marched in Columbia, the capital of South Carolina, to demand the Confederate battle flag be taken down from the state capitol. The flag had been raised over the building in 1962 by the all-white state legislature as a display of support to Jim Crow segregation and encouragement to assaults against the rising movement for Black rights. In July 2000, by vote of the state legislature, the Confederate banner was taken down and moved to a flagpole on capitol grounds next to a monument to fallen Confederate soldiers. Among the organizers of the South Carolina campaign were members of International Longshoremen's Association Local 1422 in Charleston. Three days after the January 2000 march, six hundred cops in riot gear assaulted ILA pickets at the docks protesting the use of scab labor by a shipper. Several unionists were injured, eight arrested, and five indicted on felony charges

bravely and were good men; in their big majority they were the sons of workers and farmers, like most soldiers in any modern army. What does that have to do with the murderous political meaning of the battle flag of the Confederate army, an army defeated and crushed for all time 136 years ago?

Displayed today, that flag is an emblem of, and encouragement to, reactionary forces who are determined to preserve as much as they can of the consequences of a bloody counterrevolution that shaped the trajectory of the U.S. class struggle in the twentieth century—and who are acting on that determination. It is a symbol of the fight by deadly enemies of labor to turn back the gains of the civil rights movement and to divide and weaken the working class in this country. It is the banner under which, only a few years ago, brutal and bloody assaults against Blacks were launched. And, most important, it remains a banner under which such racist assaults often *are* and *will be* launched until the capitalist roots of that Dixie rag are ripped out by the toilers of this country and replaced by the dictatorship of the proletariat.

Class-conscious workers and farmers always strive to function in the present as history. We don't approach the present as simply a *moment*. We don't approach social phe-

---

of instigating a riot. A month before the conference where the talk published here was given, five thousand unionists and supporters—including workers involved in other strikes and labor battles—marched and rallied in Columbia to demand, "Free the Charleston Five!" In November 2001 prosecutors dropped the frame-up felony charges and replaced them with misdemeanors, to which the workers pled no contest and were fined $100 each.

In April 2001 a ballot proposition to keep the Mississippi state flag, which features the Confederate battle flag, was adopted by a 2–1 vote in a statewide referendum.

nomena and political activity like a collection of snapshots to look at, one by one by one. To do so would mean bowing to the pragmatism instilled in the consciousness of working people by the very operations and history of the capitalist system in the United States, a pragmatism that guides the functioning of the bourgeoisie itself. The last thing workers and farmers are supposed to do in this country is to think in historic—contradictory and complex—terms let alone act on this understanding. All the history we're supposed to know and believe in can be boiled down to this: "America is the land of opportunity. If you work hard and stay out of trouble, you can get ahead and maybe get a business and hire some workers yourself some day." That's it.

We are often involved in battles that go back generations—whether it's a struggle by Black farmers, or a fight by coal miners or uranium miners to defend hard-won union rights and government-funded medical benefits, or decades-long battles around textile mills or packing plants. Whenever we do find ourselves in the midst of such battles, we should take special pleasure in these experiences and draw from them everything we can. Among other reasons, knowledge of that living history can be a source of proletarian humility—as well as a reminder of our responsibility. Because it helps workers such as ourselves and others understand that individual actions don't count for much unless they are part of a sustained, disciplined, and collective effort over time. And that irresponsibility or indiscipline today also results in a needless respilling of blood already shed. Which is a high crime.

Renewing world communist movement

For the first time since the late 1920s, the communist movement has the opportunity to confront our international obligations and responsibilities in a world in which our efforts are no longer obstructed by the enormous power of the Stalinist world apparatuses and the wholesale confusion of communism with Stalinism. This presents new political openings, the scope of which we can only grasp over time and in the doing.

Only with the victory of the Bolsheviks in October 1917 did the world as a whole become an arena for practical party organizing by communists. With that victory the construction of communist parties began being posed in one country after another, in every part of the world. The task was to recruit the cadres and forge the leaderships of proletarian parties capable of organizing workers and farmers to follow the example of the Bolsheviks. The most class-conscious, selfless, and politically competent workers and farmers were won to national sections of the Communist International—both in the imperialist countries, and in the oppressed nations fighting for their liberation from imperialist domination. Revolutionary-minded youth from all backgrounds were politically attracted to the selfless proletarian road. Inspired by the political intransigence and self-sacrifice of the Bolshevik-led workers and peasants of the young Soviet republic, they were won to spreading its example and emulating its deeds worldwide.

The three-year-long civil war launched by the defeated capitalists and landlords, backed up by imperialist armies, however, took an enormous toll on the vanguard of the working class, as well as on toilers in city and countryside across the young Soviet republic. The death and destruction coincided with the defeat of revolutions in Germany and Hungary, as well as the crushing of a prerevolutionary wave of factory occupations in Italy. By the mid-1920s, following Lenin's death, both the party and state in the Soviet Union and the leadership of the Communist International had begun to come under the domination of an expanding privileged social caste, a process consolidated by the closing years of that decade. This Stalinist officialdom increasingly pursued counterrevolutionary policies that subordinated the struggles of workers and peasants both at home and abroad to maintaining the relative privileges of the bureaucratic caste, as it subordinated the toilers' revolutionary needs to the narrowing national goals of Russian diplomacy. It turned on those who fought to continue the proletarian internationalist course of Lenin and the Bolsheviks, drove the weakest and most vulnerable out of revolutionary politics, and in the 1930s unleashed a terror campaign of purge trials, executions, labor camps, and assassinations that decimated vanguard proletarian forces.

U<small>NDER STALINIST</small> domination, the leadership of the Communist International became, in Leon Trotsky's words, both an organizer of defeats—in China, in Germany, in France, in Spain, and elsewhere—and of an international murder machine. Outside the Soviet Union, the victims of Stalin's secret police were first and foremost the communist vanguard of worker, peasant, and national liberation struggles around the world.

Throughout this period, however, the parties of the Communist International continued to attract and win the big majority of the most seasoned fighters among working people and the oppressed worldwide. The international revolutionary movement would have suffered a much less devastating blow had the Stalinists openly rejected Marxism, stopped calling themselves communists, and ceased identifying themselves with Lenin and his course and with defense of the conquests of the October Revolution. But that's not what happened. The bureaucratic caste "cowed the revolutionary vanguard, trampled upon Marxism, prostituted the Bolshevik Party," as Trotsky put it in 1937.[31]

The Stalinists not only remained the officialdom of the Soviet workers state and party, but pretended to be the authentic bearers of the continuity of Bolshevism. They needed this cover, since they could not state what they actually were: a parasitic bureaucracy; an unnecessary obstacle to the advance of labor productivity in city and countryside in the Soviet Union; a betrayer of revolutionary forces abroad whenever that served their narrow national and diplomatic interests; an international instrument of thuggery against communist challengers; an ideology and apparatus with no necessary historical function.

Revolutionary-minded workers, farmers, and young people attracted to Marxism and looking for a party to help them fight more effectively continued pouring into the ranks of the Communist Parties in the late 1920s and 1930s. Only a relative handful of CP cadres such as Jim Cannon and others charted a proletarian road, independent of the needs of the Stalinist apparatus in Moscow and abroad, to continue Lenin's course. That is the source of the communist continuity of the Socialist Workers Party—from Marx and Engels, to the Bolshevik movement in Lenin's time, to this day.

Some CP members in the late 1920s and 1930s left the parties demoralized and either dropped out of political activity or drifted into bourgeois trade unionism or bour-

31. Leon Trotsky, "Stalinism and Bolshevism," in *Writings of Leon Trotsky (1936–37)* (New York: Pathfinder, 1970, 1978), p. 537 [2012 printing]. Hereafter, *Trotsky Writings*.

geois politics of one or another variety. But many stayed in the Stalinist organizations for various periods of time and sought to rationalize each new betrayal and crime as it came along. They couldn't look in a mirror and admit to themselves what had become of the movement they had organized their lives to build and advance. And neither they nor their children ever will.

I hope conference participants take the opportunity to see the movie *Terrorists in Retirement* that we'll be showing several times during the conference. It tells the story of a number of emigrant Communists from Eastern Europe, most of them Jewish, who became part of the antifascist resistance movement in Paris during World War II. One of the things to notice in the film—and you'll be struck by many other insights into Stalinism too, if you're paying close attention—are the accounts by these workers (most of them garment workers, by the way) of how they sought to rationalize all sorts of things that were happening to them and all around them whose implications they feared to face. How they initially tried to turn a blind eye even to the nationalist treachery of the Stalinist misleaders of the French Resistance who didn't lift a finger to protect these foreign-born cadres during the war, and who afterwards refused to acknowledge their contributions and sacrifices. Many decades later, a few of these workers—all of them by then in their sixties and seventies—were still hunting in the back of their minds to find a way somehow to rationalize these events, to rationalize their own political lives.

As a result of what I've been describing here, several generations of revolutionary-minded working people were broken politically by the Stalinist movement. They were destroyed as proletarian revolutionists and could not be won to communism. And their "continuity"—one based ultimately on force exerted from Moscow or Beijing, not on a proletarian program—is today disappearing into the darkness.

What was opened by the Cuban Revolution

During the half decade following World War II, workers and peasants revolutions in China, Korea, Vietnam, Yugoslavia, and Albania, together with the overturn of capitalist social relations in a number of other Eastern and Central European countries, began placing some limits on the ability of Moscow and the parties subservient to it to function as they had for the previous two decades. The monolithic character of world Stalinism started fracturing. These sharp and sometimes violent conflicts among rival "national communisms," however, did not mark an advance for building a revolutionary proletarian movement—whatever initial hopes were held and efforts extended in defense of the Yugoslav, Chinese, and Vietnamese revolutions.

Something fundamental changed, however, with the victory of the Cuban Revolution in January 1959. We've talked and written about the significance of that revolution many times before, but let me discuss it today from a particular angle. That is, the victory in Cuba came at a time when the Soviet workers state was still strong enough to provide substantial military and economic help to a revolutionary government that was an enemy of Washington, insofar as Moscow considered doing so to be in its diplomatic interests. At the same time, the revolution triumphed at a moment when the world Stalinist movement had become weakened enough that its murder machine was no longer able to respond to threats to its domination, from those charting a proletarian internationalist course, by organizing successfully to eliminate Fidel Cas-

tro, Raúl Castro, Che Guevara, and other central leaders of the July 26 Movement, Rebel Army, and the forces
directly linked to them. The Stalinists weren't able to do
in Cuba what they had done so often before—and were
to succeed in doing again some two decades later, when
they murdered Maurice Bishop and destroyed the Grenada Revolution. The Stalinist movement was too weak
and the revolutionary leadership in Cuba too capable.

It's not that the Stalinists didn't try. They did. They
made their move in the opening years of the Cuban
Revolution—in 1962, and again in 1968. But the faction
around Aníbal Escalante—a central leader of the old Stalinist Popular Socialist Party (PSP), who had been named
organization secretary of the new, fused revolutionary
party—proved too weak to pull it off, even with international backing brokered through the Czech embassy in
Havana. We've written about this many times.[32] Nobody
can prove the "microfaction," as they are called in Cuba,
would have killed Fidel, and Raúl, and Che had the relationship of forces been different. But the historical record
does show that Cuban leaders weren't going to stand by
in face of a counterrevolutionary coup from within and
allow the workers and peasants to be led to defeat.

The revolutionary course of the leadership in Cuba was
a decisive turning point for prospects to renew the international communist movement. Today, a little more than
forty years after it conquered, the Cuban Revolution has not

---

32. See Jack Barnes, "The Fight for a Workers' and Farmers' Government in the United States" in *New International* no. 4 (1985),
pp. 270–74 [2008 printing]; and the section "A Lesson from the
Cuban Revolution" in Steve Clark, "The Second Assassination
of Maurice Bishop" in *New International* no. 6 (1987), pp. 110–18
[2007 printing].

merely "survived." It continues to act as, and to be, a revolutionary and internationalist example for working people around the world, including here in the United States.

Revolutionary continuity and our proletarian heritage

The disintegration of the international Stalinist movement has reached the point where it no longer does the one thing that for decades added a gloss of authenticity to its false claim to be the bearer of communist continuity: it no longer even publishes the works of Marx, Engels, and Lenin. Or much of anything else political for that matter. There is no longer a Russian, or German, or Chinese party that puts resources into promoting and selling programmatic books and pamphlets, let alone using them as indirect subsidies to foreign favorites. Even when the Stalinist movement did produce this literature, of course, its aim was never to educate and politically arm new generations of proletarian revolutionists. That point is graphically underlined by one of the displays at the back of the conference hall, which everyone here should take the opportunity to enjoy and learn from over the next few days. The display put together by the Pathfinder Reprint Project volunteers includes the beautiful cover of Pathfinder's *Lenin's Final Fight*, with a big arrow labeled: "This is a book that wants to be read." Next to it is the ugly, stock reddish cover of the final Soviet-produced edition of Lenin's *What Is To Be Done?*, with an arrow saying: "This book screams, 'Don't read me!' "

Perfect. Those books *weren't* meant to be read. They were produced as part of the litany in the vulgar tongues. They could only be understood by the laity through interpretations anointed, and periodically changed, by Moscow (or Beijing). They were the sacred chants from the choir, while the Word was handed down from the altar:

the rationalizations for the class-collaborationist Popular Front course, for the Moscow Trials, for the Stalin-Hitler pact, for being the most brutal enforcers of the no-strike pledges during World War II, for clinking champagne glasses with Nixon while bombs were raining down on Vietnam, for betraying Che and Fidel's revolutionary initiative in Bolivia, for campaigning for Lyndon Johnson, or whatever.

Unattractive as these books and pamphlets were, they were ornamental in purpose. Form followed function. They were not intended to attract groups of rank-and-file workers, of worker-bolsheviks to read, discuss, and internalize them as a guide to political action. The display prepared by the reprint project volunteers says the simple truth: these books were not made for workers; they were made for the record.

We, on the other hand, put such effort and resources into making our books and pamphlets attractive and readable because we're determined to get them to the growing numbers of vanguard workers, farmers, and youth who want them and need them. We're proud of them. We build bridges to reading and understanding them: photo sections that are painstakingly researched and imaginatively designed; striking front covers, sometimes including the decorative incorporation of works of art; careful attention to presentation of the text. None of these are monopolies of the ruling rich.

Even the "plain brown wrapper" editions of Marxist classics are largely no longer being produced by the decomposing Stalinist movement, however. In the United States this goes back a few years, even before Gus Hall's replacement as CP national chairman by Sam Webb in early 2000 and Hall's death a short while later. In a 1996 report to the party's national leadership published in its monthly magazine, *Political Affairs,* Hall lamented that, "The whole truth about our beautiful bookstore [on 23rd Street in Lower Manhattan] has to include the fact that it does not make a profit. It does not pay rent. . . . It does not contribute to the financial well-being of our Party." As for International Publishers itself, Hall said, "Notwithstanding the importance and benefits of having a Party publishing house, the fact is the Party does not get any financial benefits." Alas, Moscow's subsidies were no more!

Open flight from 'What Is To Be Done?'

This trend has accelerated under Webb, who has organized the CPUSA's leading bodies to reject what he calls the "doctrinal purity" and "pat answers of yesterday," when the party's course was still shaped by "the sectarian policies of the Communist movement in its formative period." For the first time, the CP is today overtly shunting Marx, Engels, and Lenin to the side as even a ritual point of reference for political action—not just in deed, which has been the case for seventy years, but more and more in word as well. Most revealing, the CPUSA leadership doesn't organize Young Communist League members to read basics of Marxism.

Webb, for example, openly rejects Lenin's insistence in *What Is To Be Done?,* and throughout his writings, that the working class cannot develop communist ideas simply from its own experiences and lessons in a particular industry, a particular region or country, or even a series of hard-fought class battles. In doing so, Webb rejects one of the central political foundations of Bolshevism. He openly denies that proletarian class consciousness has to be brought into the fighting working-class vanguard by a communist party that is engaged as part of the struggles unfolding along lines of proletarian resistance to the imperialist rulers and that is generalizing the lessons of working-class battles from the past one hundred and fifty years, lessons from all over the world. He denies that such a party must be constantly analyzing and explaining the relations among *all* the classes in capitalist society as a guide to its own independent *working-class* course. In short, on the centenary of *What Is To Be Done?*, the CPUSA has decreed that it belongs in the wastebasket, not just yellowing on a shelf.

The truth, however, is that Lenin's point is as decisive for communists today as ever. Petty-bourgeois radicals have often tried to twist what Lenin was saying into an assertion that people such as themselves—those from the middle class—must bring revolutionary ideas to the working class. But that is a self-serving falsification. At the opening of the twentieth century, Lenin confronted growing reformist and trade-unionist currents in the leadership of the revolutionary workers movement in Russia. In face of that, he forcefully reasserted the political heart of the Communist Manifesto: that communists have no historic interests separate and apart from those of the proletariat as a whole. That our program and strategy, as the Manifesto puts it, "merely express, in general terms, actual relations springing from an existing class struggle, from a historical movement going on under our very eyes." And that communists, therefore, "have over the great mass of the proletariat the advantage of clearly understanding the line of march, the conditions, and the ultimate general results of the proletarian movement," leading to the revolutionary conquest of power by the working class.[33]

That's Lenin's point: the need for a communist party

33. Marx and Engels, *The Communist Manifesto*, p. 47.

that is part and parcel of the mass vanguard of the working class in action, and that brings revolutionary political consciousness into it. The need for a disciplined party that can help workers see and understand struggles taking place and challenges existing in the industry, the region, and the country in which they live, work, and fight *as part of the world,* and as part of an *ongoing* history. As the size and social weight of the working class grows relative to other classes, as it has over the past century, this job can and will be done by parties that are increasingly proletarian in the composition of their membership and leadership. In the United States a higher and higher percentage of the leadership of the revolutionary party will be workers, unlike the central leadership of most Marxist parties up to this point in history.

Cumulative lessons of 150 years of working-class movement

Today, when a worker, a farmer, or a young person gets involved in struggles and becomes interested in broader ideas, the place to look for Marxism is no longer a party subordinate to the Stalinist caste and its institutions in the Soviet Union, or China. That's not where militants will get the books and pamphlets that not only can open up an entire new world for them, but also present the proletarian message of how to change that world. All the experience and leadership lessons the communist movement has accumulated over decades in building a proletarian party, all the political work we've done to record the living continuity of the revolutionary workers movement, all the effort we've put into supporting a publishing house and transforming a printshop—all these accomplishments are coming to fruition in new ways.

Later in the conference Jack Willey will arrive from Algeria, returning from a three-day solidarity trip to Western Sahara during the congress of the Union of Youth of Western Sahara (UJSARIO). The week before that he had joined Jacob Perasso of the Young Socialists national leadership and Anne Howie representing the Young Socialists in the United Kingdom at the final international preparatory meeting in Algiers for the August 8–16, 15th World Festival of Youth and Students.[34]

Jack, anne, and jacob report the same kind of experience we've had at other international gatherings we've participated in over the past few years—whether a meeting of the World Federation of Democratic Youth, a solidarity conference in Cuba, or a book fair in Mexico or Tehran. Young people from all over the world who are looking for revolutionary and communist literature come to our table. They want *The Communist Manifesto, Socialism: Utopian and Scientific, State and Revolution, Imperialism: The Highest Stage of Capitalism,* and other works by Marx, Engels, and Lenin published or distributed by Pathfinder Press. They buy *Capitalism's World Disorder, Cuba and the Coming American Revolution, The Changing Face of U.S. Politics,* and a cross-section of issues of the *New International*—in all the languages we publish in. They become interested in *The History of the Russian Revolution, The Revolution Betrayed,* and *In Defense of Marxism* by Leon Trotsky. They pick up titles by Fidel Castro and Ernesto Che Guevara, and are often astounded to find books and pamphlets by Burkina Faso's Thomas Sankara and Grenada's Maurice Bishop.

---

34. Later that summer, 6,700 young people from 143 countries participated in the 15th World Festival of Youth and Students, held in Algiers.

They grab up titles by Malcolm X—literally grab them up—and we introduce them to books by James P. Cannon and Farrell Dobbs. And the list goes on and on.

We continue to reap the political rewards of the efforts we made at the opening of the 1990s to salvage so many of the volumes of the *Marx and Engels Collected Works, Lenin Collected Works,* and other Marxist classics that were otherwise on their way to the paper recyclers in the former Soviet Union to be pulped. Many of these books either don't exist any longer except for our stocks, or are virtually impossible to get hold of.

The collapse of the Stalinist parties and government apparatuses also makes it possible for us to reclaim for the communist movement a political continuity with the post–World War II revolutions in Azerbaijan, in Algeria, in Grenada, in Nicaragua, in Burkina Faso. Working people the world over also need to know and absorb the balance sheet of the rise and fall of these popular revolutionary governments that at one or another stage were not able to hold off the consequences of some combination of imperialist pressure and Stalinist betrayal. Here, too, it is the communist movement that followed these class-struggle experiences in detail, as participants and partisans. It is our movement that has recorded their lessons and the words of their leaders in order to strengthen the ability of revolutionists everywhere to identify with and make use of them in coming battles.

Understanding and retaking these revolutions as our own becomes even more important with each passing year. More and more members of the communist movement were not involved in revolutionary politics when these events occurred and have no living memory of Ahmed Ben Bella, or Maurice Bishop, or Thomas Sankara. They have no living memory of Joe Hansen's extensive reporting and analysis of the Algerian workers and farmers government in the pages of *World Outlook*,[35] or of our weekly eyewitness coverage of the Nicaraguan revolution by the *Militant* and *Perspectiva Mundial*'s Managua bureau. This will be a multifaceted learning experience.

The generations that never went through these revolutions will learn about them from the point of view of what's happening in world politics today and what communists are doing in response. The generations that did live through these events and worked together with cadres and leaders of these revolutions will relearn them together with these comrades from a different point of view.

Many young people heading to Algeria this summer for the World Youth Festival, for example, are learning for the first time about the war for national liberation waged by the Algerian people and the historic defeat they inflicted on French imperialism, culminating in independence in 1962. They are learning about the betrayals of the Algerian independence struggle by the Stalinist and Social Democratic parties in France, how the workers and farmers government headed by Ben Bella was eroded and overthrown, and how these events continue to this day to

---

35. See "The Algerian Revolution and the Character of the Ben Bella Regime" by SWP leader Joseph Hansen in *The Workers and Farmers Government* (New York: Pathfinder, 1974), pp. 19–23. Also "The Algerian Revolution from 1962 to 1969" in the same collection (pp. 67–73), and "On the Character of the Algerian Government" in Jack Barnes, *For a Workers and Farmers Government in the United States* (New York: Pathfinder, 1985), pp. 56–57. Hansen's signed and unsigned articles in the news magazine *World Outlook* can be found on microfilm at research libraries or through the inter-library loan system; ask for UMI Serials in Microform, Order Number IN6523, *Intercontinental Press*, reel no. 1 (Sept. 27, 1963–Oct. 29, 1965).

shape politics not only in Algeria but also in France.

Revolutionary-minded workers and youth from countries such as Algeria and Nicaragua and Burkina Faso and from those parts of the world—many of whom have never had access to their own history in the words of central leaders of these revolutions, or to an honest communist criticism of their trajectories—will learn the lessons of these experiences together with us. Some of them may have heard stories from family members, or from friends who are a little older. But most will never have had access to the history of their own country and its lessons first-hand, nor to the revolutionary continuity of which these struggles are part. Those we meet in factories, at plant-gate sales, at street-corner tables in workers districts, or on campuses in this country can sometimes be won to the effort to build a proletarian party to make a revolution right here in the United States.

COMMUNISTS DON'T HAVE these kinds of opportunities when our class is in the midst of a prolonged political retreat. To this day, I treasure the well-used books published in the mid-1930s and the 1940s that generous comrades in Minneapolis and Chicago and Detroit took down from their shelves and either loaned me or gave to me when I first joined the communist movement. There were some pamphlets from the 1950s as well, equally important to me, that comrades somehow had found the resources to produce. By and large, however, the party had had no publishing program for more than a decade. There was nowhere I could have bought them. Comrades in Britain, in India, and then in Ceylon had produced a few books and pamphlets by Trotsky in English that we could use, but that was about it.

That's why as opportunities opened for us in the early 1960s—as a result of the Black struggle and the Cuban Revolution, and then a growing movement against the war in Southeast Asia and a widening radicalization—the party leadership put substantial cadre and financial resources into supporting the relaunching of a publishing house and then a printshop. Today more than ever we are seeing the correctness of that decision and the leadership priority we've given to supporting and expanding that effort ever since.

We are finding a growing vanguard of workers, farmers, and youth who need these books. We're fighting alongside them in the factories, in the countryside, on picket lines, at meetings in coal mining regions, at protests against cop brutality and *la migra* raids, and elsewhere. We're meeting them around the world through our international work and the work of the other communist leagues.

They not only need the books and pamphlets the communist movement produces and distributes; they have a right to them. These books came from one place and one place only: the sweat and blood of working people such as ourselves the world over. They contain only one thing: the accumulated record and lessons of the political activities, *the political deeds,* of toilers whose past struggles give us the chance today to learn in practice and to dare the impossible—to make a revolution that opens the road to ending class exploitation and oppression for all time. A revolution on a world scale: the world that is a starting point for every perspective and task of the communist movement.

SUMMARY TALK AT CLOSING SESSION

FRENCH GOVERNMENT officials have coined a new term: they describe the United States as a "hyperpower." The term was first used by the French foreign minister last year, after which President Jacques Chirac sought to assure Washington it was not meant to be "pejorative." Chirac could have saved his assurances; the White House fellows rather liked the term.

U.S. imperialism *is* a hyperpower today. We're in no danger of losing our proletarian souls by recognizing that fact, a reality that sharpens rather than decreases the contradictions of the world capitalist order. The United States ranks first among the imperialist countries in economic power, in military might, in political reach, and—more and more so—in audacity. The U.S. rulers also harbor great illusions concerning the consequences of that audacity and its destabilizing impact on the imperialist world order.

At the closing session of the conference on June 16, 2001, Jack Barnes summarized some of the major political themes discussed during the three days. The following are major excerpts.

They might remind themselves that at the height of the grandeur of imperial Rome, the empire was already well into its decline. At the point when "the sun never set on the British empire," dusk had already begun to fall. The same is true of the American empire. Hyper or not.

During the long reign of the British empire, naval supremacy was key to its global reach and power. Since World War II the U.S. Navy—with its aircraft carriers, battle groups, and nuclear-armed and nuclear-powered submarines—has ruled the waves. Washington's ability to dominate the skies has become more and more decisive, as well.

Today imperialism's new ocean is space. We're not talking about the future; this shift in theater is already under way. The White House and Congress are working to deploy the initial stages of NMD—their National Missile Defense system. After Reagan's "Star Wars" program was shelved in the late 1980s, the Clinton administration revived it less than a decade later with plans for an initially land-based system in Alaska. Bush is now pressing ahead with the control center and missile silos in Alaska, while proposing to spend in the range of $8 billion on developing and deploying an air-, sea-, and space-based "missile shield."[36]

The U.S. rulers' longer-run aim is not only to deploy a so-called missile defense system in space, but to seed the

---

36. The U.S. government loaded the first ground-based missile interceptor into a silo in Alaska in July 2004. President Bush hailed the installation as "the beginning of a missile-defense system that was envisioned by Ronald Reagan." A spokesperson for Democrat John Kerry said that while the party's presidential candidate considered missile defense "crucial to our national security strategy," funding priority should first be given to Kerry's proposal to expand the U.S. armed forces by 40,000 troops.

heavens with ballistic missiles. They are already deploy-ing a large spying apparatus "in the blue." That will top off their existing land, sea, and air power—"Full Spec-trum Dominance," as the Defense Department straight-forwardly describes it. Their goal is a nuclear capacity enabling them to blackmail any government on earth, including those with their own strategic nuclear arse-nals and delivery systems—that is, Russia, France, and the United Kingdom. Israel, and by then perhaps China, might squeak into that category, too. Plus Pakistan and India, and maybe the Democratic People's Republic of Korea, Iran, and who else? While this is the U.S. rulers' long-range plan, attaining it is a good ways off. But they have more immediate and politically important goals that are part of it.

Washington is training its sights on the workers states in China and north Korea. Both Beijing and Pyong-yang, in order to defend themselves in face of the U.S. government's massive military might in the Pacific and Asia, are buying, stealing, cobbling together, and develop-ing their own ballistic missiles that are becoming more powerful, more accurate, and longer range. The U.S. rul-ers have a bead on Iraq, on Iran, and on other countries in the Middle East. They continue to target Russia, but Washington recognizes that Moscow does not have the economic resources today to stanch the rapid degrada-tion of its *current* military power, let alone hold its own in any nuclear arms race.

Ultimately, the American rulers are even aiming at those who in their big majority have been lulled for de-cades—although never everybody—into believing the dream (the hope) that they couldn't possibly ever be a target: the strongest of Washington's rival imperialist allies in Western Europe.

Japan, as we are all reminded each August, is less sanguine.

The French, German, and other competitors of U.S. finance capital in Western Europe have no illusion they can counter Washington's militarization drive on the same plane. Instead, their plan is to try to put together a confederal setup of some sort within Europe, enabling them to better bargain with the United States. The obstacle to achieving such unity is their own rivalries, which will sharpen. The recognition of their own vulnerabilities and efforts to do something about them are far from irrational on the part of the various ruling classes in Europe. To bring a "new Europe" *into being*, however, is another matter. That is already fraught with conflicts that will become increasingly volatile and destabilizing, and, as that occurs, the class struggle across the continent and beyond will be accelerated. As "Europe" grows, it will become even less a unit.

If you include the candidates under consideration for entry into the European Union over the next few years, the EU could have as many as twenty-seven members, up from fifteen today. Current members range from the most industrially advanced capitalist countries such as Germany, France, and the United Kingdom, to countries with large pockets of more economically underdeveloped regions such as Portugal, Greece, and Ireland. And it is slated to include states in Central and Eastern Europe where capitalism's popularity is skin deep and yet to be tested in war or depression.[37]

---

37. In May 2004, ten additional governments were admitted to the European Union: Estonia, Latvia, and Lithuania, former repub-

Given these economic, social, and political disparities—and with rivalry over markets for commodities, capital, and labor among the separate national capitalist classes—intensifying conflicts are built into any effort over time to maintain a common monetary policy governing the new euro currency.[38]

WHILE A NUMBER of governments around the world are likely to increase the share of euros in their foreign exchange reserves, neither in Europe nor anywhere else does finance capital have confidence in the prospect of a strong euro as good as the dollar, let alone as good as gold.[39] Central banks around the globe, especially in Asia, continue to buy up hundreds of billions of dollars in U.S.

---

lics of the Soviet Union; the Czech Republic, Hungary, Poland, Slovakia, and Slovenia; and Malta and Cyprus. The average per capita national income of these ten countries is less than half that of the other fifteen.

38. Between 1999 and 2002, twelve European Union members replaced their national currencies with a single currency called the euro, but motion toward adoption of the euro seems to have peaked. Government-backed proposals to join the currency union were defeated in referenda in Denmark in September 2000 and Sweden in September 2003. British prime minister Anthony Blair, who backs euro adoption, indefinitely postponed a referendum, saying in April 2004 that he couldn't "make a compelling case, economically, for Britain to get into the single currency."

39. The euro's share of world foreign currency reserves rose from 15.9 percent in 2000 to 18.7 percent at the end of 2002, while the dollar's share fell from 67.5 percent to 64.5 percent. As of September 2003, however, more than 80 percent of European exports to the United States, and 90 percent of U.S. exports to Europe, were still being invoiced in dollars.

Treasury bonds to secure their hard currency reserves and facilitate their export offensive. That accounts for the strength of the American dollar today, and is its Achilles' heel as well. When confidence in the dollar begins to erode, the pricking of this bond bubble will magnify the crisis of U.S. capitalism, with repercussions the world over. But it won't eliminate the contradictions over paper currencies within "Euroland"; it will sharpen them.

While we've been meeting here this week, Bush's trip to Europe has dominated the media. They report that he continues to insist to his fellow heads of government that the 1972 Anti-Ballistic Missile Treaty is a dead letter. Of course, as we pointed out from day one, the ABM treaty was and has been a fake and a fraud ever since it was signed. Washington went right ahead with massive research and development on the laser systems and other technology it would use when the U.S. rulers decided they needed a missile defense system. And the terms of the treaty explicitly rejected barring the development of land-based antiballistic missiles or so-called "theater" missile defense systems covering limited geographic areas. It no more brought the world a step closer to peace than any of the other so-called arms limitations treaties signed by the U.S. and Soviet governments over the past several decades—or "disarmament pacts" that have been so solemnly sworn to by bourgeois powers, and so despised by revolutionary Marxists, since the closing decades of the nineteenth century.

Instead, the offer Bush has made in Europe this week— and that he'll present to Russian president Vladimir Putin when they meet in Slovenia tomorrow—is a major cut in the U.S. stockpile of nuclear warheads. Bush proposes slashing the U.S. nuclear arsenal to 2,000 warheads or even less, from the current level of more than 7,000. All the better if Moscow agrees to do the same, Bush says, but Washington will begin unilateral reductions either way.[40] That will still leave Washington with enough warheads and missiles to destroy any enemy many times over.

This proposal shouldn't surprise us. Bush is following in the steps of President Ronald Reagan, who made an even more sweeping proposal to Mikhail Gorbachev during the 1986 summit meeting in Reykjavik, Iceland. If Moscow would drop its objections to U.S. deployment of the Star Wars ABM system, Reagan said, then Washington would agree to the mutual elimination of all nuclear warheads over a ten-year period and share the ABM system with Moscow. The deal never went anywhere. The decomposition of the Soviet bureaucracy was already too advanced for Gorbachev to risk the opposition he would face by agreeing to ABM deployment, and the White House quickly dismissed the initiative as an "inaccurate interpretation" of what Reagan had proposed. Instead, the following year the U.S. and Soviet governments signed an agreement eliminating an entire class of missiles from Western and Eastern Europe. But it's been clear ever since that sooner or later a U.S. administration would put some version of that proposal back on the table.

BUSH EMBARRASSES many of the European prime ministers and presidents by saying openly that the 1997 Kyoto Protocol on air pollution and climate control is a

---

40. In 2003 both the U.S. Senate and the Russian Duma ratified the Strategic Offensive Reductions Treaty, signed by Bush and Putin in May 2002. The treaty calls for each government to reduce the number of deployed nuclear warheads to between 1,700 and 2,200 by the end of 2012.

fake and a fraud, too. Bush does so in order to rationalize the bipartisan course of the U.S. rulers, which is to place profits ahead of public health and safety, as well as protection of the environment. But the simple fact is, once again, that the Kyoto Protocol *is* a fake and a fraud. No imperialist government has any intention of sacrificing profitability in order to stay within the quotas assigned to them for the emission of carbon dioxide or other greenhouse gases. The treaty is written to allow the wealthiest governments to purchase or trade emission rights to expand their quotas, while the burden falls on semicolonial countries that can't afford to buy their way out.

This morning's papers report on Bush's speech in Poland yesterday at the University of Warsaw. Pointing to the next NATO summit meeting in a year and a half, scheduled for the end of 2002, Bush urged favorable consideration of requests for admission by ten Central and Eastern European countries formerly members of the Soviet-initiated Warsaw Pact. "All of Europe's new democracies, from the Baltic to the Black Sea and all that lie between, should have the same chance for security and freedom—and the same chance to join the institutions of Europe—as Europe's old democracies have," said Bush. "I believe in NATO membership for all of Europe's democracies that seek it and are ready to share the responsibilities that NATO brings. The question of 'when' may still be up for debate; the question of 'whether' should not be."[41]

---

41. In March 2004, NATO admitted seven additional countries: Estonia, Latvia, and Lithuania (former Soviet republics); Bulgaria, Romania, and Slovakia (former Warsaw Pact members); and Slovenia, previously a republic of Yugoslavia. The Czech Republic, Hungary, and Poland, also former Warsaw Pact members, had been admitted to NATO in 1999.

Then Bush held out to Putin the prospect of a cooperative Russia being included under the protection of the U.S.-dominated NATO military alliance in Europe and receiving economic assistance from Wall Street's rivals across the Atlantic. "The Europe we are building must also be open to Russia," Bush said. "We have a stake in Russia's success—and we look for the day when Russia is fully reformed, fully democratic and closely bound to the rest of Europe. Europe's great institutions—NATO and the European Union—can and should build partnerships with Russia and with all the countries that have emerged from the wreckage of the former Soviet Union."

"Russia is part of Europe," Bush added, "and, therefore, does not need a buffer zone of insecure states separating it from Europe." The chief executive of the U.S. imperialist government also made it crystal clear who should pick up the tab for this broad vision: "Across the region, nations are yearning to be part of Europe," he said. "The burdens—and benefits—of satisfying that yearning will naturally fall most heavily on Europe itself."

AS CRISES-FUELED TENSIONS mount among European governments themselves, these conflicts will be exacerbated by U.S. finance capital. Washington will continue not only to strengthen its long-standing "special relationship" with London. It will bolster other old alliances as it forges new links with governments across the continent, including in Eastern and Central Europe, and seeks to play to its advantage the lines of cleavage that will emerge and deepen. Thus the seeds of sharpening and accelerating interimperialist conflict continue to be sown in "Europe."

Communists insist that every social and political question is a class question. We reject any call to act on behalf of "the nation" in an imperialist country. We deny there are military, environmental, or any other questions where the consequences are "just too horrible," or the technical issues "too complex," for the proletariat to advance a course in the class interests of the exploited and oppressed.

There is no social or political question that can be extracted from history, looked at through a microscope, and then resolved in the interests "of all," irrespective of class position. There are no questions facing humanity that hover above class politics. All "technical" or "scientific" questions related to energy production, the instruments of war, or social policy will be resolved through the capitalist market in combination with the state power that acts on behalf of the capitalist class. That will only change when the working class has led a revolution to take state power out of the hands of that tiny wealthy minority. Along that line of march the proletariat can and will wrest real concessions as by-products of its revolutionary struggle.

Human labor is social labor. Its product is not the result of the work of an individual, nor even the work of many individuals summed together. Something can seem to be an individual act: putting in a field of corn, making a pair of shoes, operating a machine, and so on. That labor, however, is always surrounded by, and dependent upon, a web of social relations, however directly or indirectly. What happens to the product of that farmer, that shoemaker, that worker is determined by the class relations under which they toil. It is social labor that bequeaths generation after generation the culture, the blueprints, to transform material reality in new and more productive ways and to make possible the creation of a better world.

Marx polemicized against those in the workers movement of his day who presented the unscientific view that labor is the source of all wealth. "Labor is *not the source* of all wealth," he insisted in 1875. "*Nature* is just as much the source of use values . . . as labor, which itself is only the manifestation of a force of nature, human labor power." By the very fact that labor depends upon land and natural resources in the production process, Marx said, workers—who have no property other than their own labor power—become under the capitalist system "the slave of other men who have made themselves the owners of the material conditions of labor."[42] That private ownership of land, of the means of production, and of raw materials is the basis of both the economic and state power of the capitalist class.

At the same time, Marx wrote in *Capital*, the capitalist class, in its competition for profits, only develops the techniques and social process of production—both in industry and in agriculture—"by simultaneously undermining the original sources of all wealth—the soil and the worker."[43] The logic of the capitalist system, Marx and Engels taught us, is, over time, to transform the forces of production into forces of destruction. History has confirmed the accuracy of that observation, to the nth degree.

Once we understand this reality, however, the only thing that should be scary to any of us is the prospect of *not* organizing ourselves as part of a disciplined compo-

---

42. Marx, "Critique of the Gotha Programme," in *MECW*, vol. 24, p. 81.

43. Marx, *Capital*, vol. 1, p. 638.

nent of a working-class vanguard to prevent such an outcome. And that requires a program and strategy to close
the gap produced and reproduced by imperialism in the
social and cultural conditions of toilers in countries at
different stages of economic and social development the
world over. To work toward the convergence of the conditions of life within the only force on earth that can carry
out successful revolutionary struggles along the line of
march of the proletariat toward political power. So long
as the vanguard of the working class doesn't do what the
exploiters try to scare and bribe them into doing—recoil
in fear from that task—the transformation of nature in
a sustainable and renewable way opens an unbounded
future for humanity.

That's what the constitution of the Socialist Workers
Party reminds us: that the purpose of the party is not
to build "American" socialism, but to educate and organize the working class to take power here and join in the
worldwide struggle for socialism. Our goal is to bring the
mighty weight of a popular revolutionary government in
the United States into the international socialist revolution. Just think about what Cuban workers and farmers
have done since making a socialist revolution—in a semicolonial country with a population of some seven million
people in 1959. They lifted the world on their shoulders.
Then think about what the toilers could use Soviet power
in the United States to accomplish.

REVOLUTIONISTS WHO LIVE and work in the United
States carry out our political activity not only in the
wealthiest country on earth, but in one that has not experienced war on its own soil since 1865. It is a country in
which there have been bloody class battles and proletarian

social movements, but there has never been a revolutionary situation or workers' insurrection. It is a country that has seen genocidal treatment of native populations and organized murderous violence over decades by reactionary outfits such as the Ku Klux Klan, as well as systematic brutality by cops, National Guardsmen, and employer goons—but has experienced only limited combat in the streets and on the picket lines between fascist gangs and defense guards of labor and the oppressed.

So communists in the United States have a special need and a special responsibility to understand and explain the economic and social realities facing the vast majority of humanity and our place in that humanity, a place ultimately determined *by* that humanity. We confront our revolutionary tasks, as Lenin and the Bolsheviks taught us, in an imperialist world divided between the oppressed nations of Asia, Africa, and the Americas, and a handful of oppressor nations. We are still living in the epoch of imperialist conflicts and world wars, colonial uprisings, civil wars, and revolutions.

We never begin as "Americans" in anything we do. We begin as a part of the workers of the world, the part in "America." We begin as soldiers of the world revolution. That's the only "we" that communists know.

$\mathit{Building\ a}$ PROLETARIAN PARTY

Lenin's Final Fight
Speeches and Writings, 1922–23
V.I. LENIN

In 1922 and 1923, V.I. Lenin, central leader of the world's first socialist revolution, waged what was to be his last political battle. At stake was whether that revolution, and the international movement it led, would remain on the proletarian course that had brought workers and peasants to power in October 1917. Indispensable to understanding the world class struggle in the 20th and 21st centuries. $20. Also in Spanish.

Their Trotsky and Ours
JACK BARNES

To lead the working class in a successful revolution, a mass proletarian party is needed whose cadres, well beforehand, have absorbed a world communist program, are proletarian in life and work, derive deep satisfaction from doing politics, and have forged a leadership with an acute sense of what to do next. This book is about building such a party. $16. Also in Spanish and French.

The History of American Trotskyism, 1928–1938
Report of a Participant
JAMES P. CANNON

"Trotskyism is not a new movement, a new doctrine," Cannon says, "but the restoration, the revival of genuine Marxism as it was expounded and practiced in the Russian revolution and in the early days of the Communist International." In twelve talks given in 1942, Cannon recounts a decisive period in efforts to build a proletarian party in the United States. $22. Also in Spanish and French.

What Is To Be Done?
V.I. LENIN

The stakes in creating a disciplined organization of working-class revolutionaries capable of acting as a "tribune of the people, able to react to every manifestation of tyranny and oppression, no matter where it appears, to clarify for all and everyone the world-historic significance of the struggle for the emancipation of the proletariat." Written in 1902. In *Essential Works of Lenin.* $12.95

In Defense of Marxism
Against the Petty-Bourgeois Opposition in the Socialist Workers Party
LEON TROTSKY

Writing in 1939–40, Leon Trotsky replies to those in the revolutionary workers movement beating a retreat from defense of the Soviet Union in face of the looming imperialist assault. Why only a party that fights to bring growing numbers of workers into its ranks and leadership can steer a steady revolutionary course. $25. Also in Spanish.

The Struggle for a Proletarian Party
JAMES P. CANNON

"The workers of America have power enough to topple the structure of capitalism at home and to lift the whole world with them when they rise," Cannon asserts. On the eve of World War II, a founder of the communist movement in the US and leader of the Communist International in Lenin's time defends the program and party-building norms of Bolshevism. $22

Revolutionary Continuity
Marxist Leadership in the U.S.
FARRELL DOBBS

How successive generations took part in struggles of the US labor movement, seeking to build a leadership that could advance the class interests of workers and small farmers and link up with fellow toilers around the world. Two volumes:

The Early Years, 1848–1917, $20; *Birth of the Communist Movement, 1918–1922,* $19.

OUR POLITICS START WITH THE WORLD
Conference Question and Answer Session

QUESTION: You spoke this morning about the new book, *Cuba and the Coming American Revolution*. The second part of that book is based on talks you gave a few months ago in Seattle and New York. There's a sentence in there that I don't understand, or perhaps I don't agree with. You're describing the changes in the working class and labor movement in the United States, along the lines you've also done here, and you say: "The pace of the manifestations of this sea change in the class struggle, of course, goes through ebbs and flows. Resistance speeds up and broadens for a while, and then slows down." Then you add—and this is the sentence I question—"The unions, the sole mass institutions of the American labor movement today, continue to weaken."

At the international socialist conference in Oberlin, Ohio, June 14–16, 2001, an afternoon discussion session followed the opening talk by Jack Barnes, "Our Politics Start with the World," published on the preceding pages. Several of the questions raised issues frequently asked by revolutionary-minded working people and youth who become interested in the activities and perspectives of the communist movement. Printed here are two of those exchanges.

You go on: "The traditions promoted by the union officialdom—a product of their bourgeois outlook and values, and their petty-bourgeois conditions of life—leave them utterly unready for what can suddenly erupt under the current crises-ridden conditions of world capitalism. Above all they are unprepared for the struggles building up underneath, not to mention frightened by that prospect. They, too, can never understand the capacities of the ranks."

Well, everyone at this conference can agree with what you say here about the labor officialdom. But it doesn't seem to me that a continued weakening of the unions necessarily flows from that. When communists talk about the unions getting stronger, don't we mean that the ranks are gaining confidence and becoming more involved in the union? And isn't that what has been happening over the past year or so? For example, there's been the recent contract won through a two-and-a-half-month strike by garment workers at Hollander Home Fashions in Los Angeles and Frackville, Pennsylvania, with workers at the Tignall, Georgia, plant honoring their picket lines and refusing to work. For the first time in years the United Mineworkers is actually on a serious drive to organize nonunion mines. There are the United Food and Commercial Workers organizing drives among packinghouse workers in the Midwest, led in many cases by immigrant workers. So, could you explain what you meant when you said that the unions continue to get weaker today?

Unions continue to weaken

JACK BARNES: The unions are weakening and will continue to weaken for some time. A smaller and smaller percentage of the working class is unionized. Real wages for the majority of workers continue to stagnate at best.

Speedup intensifies while job conditions deteriorate, as does the coverage and dependability of medical plans and pensions. And the employing class is chopping away at social security protections of all kinds, for the entire working class.

You're right, of course, that when workers complain about "the union" today, or about "the International," they're usually talking about an officialdom, especially the full-time staffers, organizers, and officers. So we're always looking for ways to explain to fellow fighters that the union is *us*, the membership—but by that I don't just mean the ranks; it includes the individuals in the officialdom, too. Every single paid-up member.

The bureaucracy of the AFL-CIO unions and other so-called International unions continues on its decades-long course of politically integrating the labor movement into the imperialist state apparatus. The spring issue of the *IAM Journal*, the magazine of the International Association of Machinists, for example, is emblazoned with the front-page headline "Bombs Bursting in Air" and a full-color photograph of a U.S. missile; the entire issue is devoted to the promotion, in glowing terms, of the "national missile defense system" initiated by Clinton and being pressed by Bush with substantial bipartisan support. IAM president Tom Buffenbarger extols the contribution of IAM-organized workers to building the weapons deployed by the U.S. rulers.

"Which of our cities will they target?" he writes. "In the next 15 years, rogue states with chemical, nuclear or biological weapons will also have missiles capable of reaching American cities. And the likelihood of terrorists acquiring such weapons increases by the day. Prudence dictates that we pursue a national missile defense (NMD) that works." Buffenbarger's "we" is imperialist America, and "they" are its enemies. The workers of the world aren't a factor he even considers.

And the IAM is not unique. The entire officialdom pushes patriotic campaigns to "Buy American"—whether it's steel, clothing, cars, or whatever. There is no voice charting a course for workers independent of the employers, their twin parties, and their government.

Much of the reformist and centrist left does say the unions are getting stronger. These middle-class radicals *do* identify the union with the "progressive" wing of the officialdom. They look in the mirror and see themselves reflected in the gang around John Sweeney that swept into the top positions of the AFL-CIO in 1995. These leftists flipped head over heels when that happened, and they're still dizzy. Most of them don't mention that despite Sweeney's pledge to throw the federation's resources into organizing the unorganized, union membership has continued to slide from that time to this. They will mention it. Not when they're ready to change to a proletarian perspective, but when they're ready to "back" the next Sweeney.

Even when the officialdom of one or another union does adopt a formal position in support of a demand in the interests of working people—abortion rights, amnesty for immigrants, raising the minimum wage—that only becomes useful if some group of workers grabs it and finds a way to use it to advance the struggle. Neither the labor bureaucracy itself, nor any major section of it, has any intention of throwing the weight of the unions into a social movement to fight for anything other than the protection of their own berth in capitalist society.

In *The History of American Trotskyism,* Cannon describes three strike waves during the 1930s, including several important battles in 1933—the Paterson silk strike, the beginning of the New York City hotel workers' organizing drive, and others. But the unions continued to get weaker in 1933. That only began to shift following the outcome of the strikes the next year in San Francisco, Minneapolis, and Toledo. The qualitative change came in 1936–37 with the sit-down strikes in auto and rubber and other battles that built the CIO.[44]

B
EFORE BUREAUCRATIZED unions begin to be transformed and strengthened, there has to be a broader social or political shock of some kind in the forms of the labor movement—something that presses at least sections of it toward broader layers of the working class and the oppressed. During the years of class combat that forged the industrial unions, the CIO became *a powerful social movement*. The class-struggle leadership of Teamsters Local 544, too, launched an expanding social movement that reached out to other workers in the Twin Cities and throughout the Midwest, to farmers, and to the unemployed. It fought to organize and use the power of the labor movement independent from the twin parties of the employing class, the Democrats and Republicans, to form a labor party. It campaigned to extend social security, to establish union defense guards, and to mobilize working-class opposition to imperialism and its impending world war.

Under explosive conditions such as those, strikes and related labor battles in a growing number of industries

---

44. See chapters 7 and 8, "The Turn to Mass Work" and "The Great Minneapolis Strikes," in James P. Cannon, *The History of American Trotskyism, 1928–38: Report of a Participant* (New York: Pathfinder, 1944, 2002).

or parts of the country reach a point at which the ranks are then actually able to use the unions in more and more effective ways to defend themselves and to advance the interests of the exploited and oppressed. The labor officialdom begins to divide under the pressure from below.

But this is not what's happening today in the labor movement. It's not what the sea change in resistance among layers of workers and farmers, which we consider very important politically, is about. The increasingly beleaguered union bureaucracy is being divided to some degree *from above*, under pressure from competing sections of U.S. capital—but not yet by pressure from the ranks. Stalemates or defeats still outnumber victories in strikes and organizing drives. There are significant individual successes as well, but the class struggle is still at a point where it's difficult for workers to sustain a fight to reap the fruits of those victories. It's important, however, that these situations more and more often today give rise to ongoing resistance not quick defeats, as was common for a number of years in the early and mid-1990s.

THE WORKERS AT Dakota Premium Foods in St. Paul, Minnesota, won an important union recognition vote just about exactly one year ago. Some members of UFCW Local 789 are missing a day of this conference to join in a union activity marking that anniversary. It was a strong fight, and many of the cadres remain active. But the bosses at Dakota to this day refuse to recognize the union and negotiate a contract. The fight is still on. The tone, the intensity, the relation of various fighters to each other—all this shifts over time. But the fight is still on. It is the bosses who at some stage will forget this fact—to their regret.[45]

The UNITE-organized garment workers at Hollander Home Fashions just won their strike, as mentioned by the comrade who asked the question. They turned back the employer's effort to break the union, and they forced the company to meet some of their wage and pension demands. Now they face the day-by-day challenge of holding on to those gains and laying the basis for the ongoing battle for better hours and job conditions, health and safety protections, and wages.

There is no evidence that the UMWA officialdom is on a drive today to organize nonunion coal mines. That's simply incorrect. In fact, there are no organizing *drives* anywhere in the labor movement in the United States right now. That's not the overriding priority of the officialdom of any single union.

There are some important organizing efforts going on in particular factories, mines, and worksites, and in certain cities and areas of the country. We know about a good number of them and are involved in some. We reach out to workers engaged in these organizing efforts and cover them in the *Militant* and *Perspectiva Mundial*. We work loyally with anyone who is pushing in that direction, whether they're operating a long-wall machine in a coal mine, working on the kill floor in a packinghouse, or functioning as a paid union organizer. But we and other

---

45. Through ongoing resistance over the following year—against line speedup and being made to work while injured, in defense of medical benefits, for the right to bathroom breaks, and for the bosses to abide by seniority—the workers in UFCW Local 789 forced the owners of Dakota Premium Foods to recognize the union and negotiate a contract. The agreement was approved by Local 789 members at Dakota in October 2002.

vanguard workers will know when a sustained organizing drive is launched by some section of the labor movement in this country. We won't miss it.

Preparing for coming battles

What is starting to happen is very important. We see discussion and organizing activity percolating among workers who have been pushed out of union jobs—in the mines, in a garment shop, or wherever—or whose unions have been broken over the past decade or so. We run into some of these workers when we, too, find ourselves in nonunion jobs for a period of time, or we hear about what they're doing from their friends, family members, and former co-workers. This is part of the preparation of the coming battles to transform the unions.

Both the comrades who have worked in industry for many years and comrades newer to our union fractions are together learning how to function in situations such as these and carry out competent trade union work as communists. We're having to internalize how to handle ourselves, how to avoid ultraleft errors, how to function alongside other vanguard workers on the job without getting ourselves and others victimized. Like other militants, we are going to get fired sometimes, but to get fired unnecessarily displays indisciplined functioning that harms the party, our co-workers, and the labor movement. So our fractions need to become schools of the kind of savvy functioning and communist union work that make it possible for us to be blood-and-bone of the workers whose activity today is part of the necessary preconditions for the raging battles to come.

What's so important about the end of the more-than-half-decade-long retreat by our class a few years ago is that more and more workers are refusing to be pushed back by the employers and the government without resisting. Working people make progress in a number of strikes or individual organizing drives. When hard-fought battles end in a standoff, or even in a temporary setback, fewer workers emerge permanently bitter or demoralized for long. They continue reaching out in solidarity to other workers in struggle. They remain open to ideas about how to fight more effectively and win, including to the ideas of communists they've fought alongside and come to respect. Political space in the unions opens a little more each time this occurs.

But none of this translates directly into a strengthening of the unions. That won't happen until successful battles in a number of union locals, localities, or regions begin to have a direct reflection in a new leadership whose course can be a lodestar for other workers and unionists. Until then the unions will continue to get weaker.

Unions aren't just an idea in the mind; they are institutions that actually exist and function, day in and day out, as part of capitalist society. Until the membership begins to put its stamp on those institutions—on the relations between labor and capital, the relations between labor and the entire legal structure that entangles the working class in red tape—the unions won't be strengthened. And the ranks will only place their stamp on the unions by throwing up a leadership in their locals in the course of coming struggles.

When a union struggle erupts that we're part of, all sorts of people are involved—workers, local officials, staffers. We make no prejudgments, and act on the basis of no prejudices. We work with anybody and everybody, with all our own cards face up. Sometimes local union officials hope they can ride a particular battle to a success that may redound to their personal benefit in the officialdom, and they may even smile for a time on the energy of the ranks they hope will help advance them toward that goal. But they can turn on a dime if and when that energy threatens to bring into the local leadership new forces that they do not control—let alone threatens to replace them, even if those forces don't yet have the strength to do so.

The divisions in the trade union officialdom today are the product of growing weakness, not strength. The bureaucrats are desperately trying to compensate for the continued shrinkage of their dues base, and the descent toward rock-bottom of their own influence and bargaining leverage in bourgeois politics. That's not the kind of pressure from rising rank-and-file battles that led UMWA president John L. Lewis in 1935 to break from the craft-oriented American Federation of Labor and launch the CIO.

Over the past month alone there have been several news accounts of efforts by one or another top union official to court the White House and curry favor among congressional Republicans and Democrats alike. Sweeney recently organized a dinner for seventeen Republican members of the House of Representatives. The USWA officialdom has been working overtime in Washington doing the scut work for Big Steel to win backing for substantial new tariff barriers from Bush and the Congress. The UMWA bureaucracy is praising new White House proposals to scrap environmental restrictions on coal burning and mountain-top mining. And the Teamsters union and Carpenters union officialdoms, both of which have cut loose from formal membership in the AFL-CIO, are marshaling support for big new federal construction projects promised by Bush as part of his "energy plan."

By the way, all this should lead us to be more attuned

to resistance by workers organized not just by the unions in which we have fractions, but by the Steelworkers or the Teamsters or the Carpenters or wherever. The Carpenters union is one of the few that has really grown over the past half decade—going from about 350,000 members to 550,000 members. Going back to the victory of the drywallers' strike in Los Angeles in 1992, the Carpenters have organized a substantial number of immigrant workers previously blocked out of the construction unions by the officialdom's job-trust policies. We orient to workers who are fighting, whatever union they may be organized by, or want to be organized by—the UMWA or the Carpenters, UNITE or the Teamsters, the UFCW or the Laborers. If there's a strike or an organizing drive going on, we want to be there joining in the fight and mixing it up politically with the ranks.

But we'll disarm fellow workers today if we tell them that because there's an upturn in resistance the unions are getting stronger. What communists need to point out, instead, is that by resisting the employer assaults in the way layers of workers and farmers have begun doing in recent years, we're heading up the road along which the unions can and will be strengthened. And along which, with effort and stick-to-it-iveness, class battles can be organized that will be able over time to begin transforming the unions.

THE PREPARATORY SKIRMISHES we're involved in alongside other workers today are important. In fact, without them we can't get to the next stage. Talking socialism on the job and with working people involved in struggles—signing them up as *Militant* and *PM* subscribers, discussing our books and pamphlets with them, getting them to the weekly forum or to an SWP election campaign event—that, too, is necessary. It's how we win friends, recruit, and *prepare.*

Everything we're saying here is an argument to get deeper into the unions, to strengthen our workers district branches and organizing committees, and integrate ourselves more fully into the struggles of workers and farmers across the country. Our aim is to deepen the self-confidence, the solidarity, and the political consciousness of the ranks—and to find those workers among the vanguard who will become readers of our press, come to our forums, and can be recruited to the communist party.

It's by following the actual lines of resistance among workers and farmers that seemingly out of nowhere someday we'll find ourselves involved in a vanguard struggle in which the organized power of the ranks does begin transforming a section of the labor movement somewhere—through the institutions of the unions themselves. As that happens, the unions *will* begin to get stronger, and even the political stranglehold of the imperialist two-party system choking the labor movement will start to be challenged. A whole new stage of working-class politics will open up in the United States.

QUESTION: I'm a Young Socialist from Los Angeles. This morning you said that the communist movement has an orientation toward the vanguard of the working class. I must have heard that phrase a hundred times, but I'd never really thought much before about what it meant. After the talk, I understand better how we are building the leadership of what's going to be the future communist movement in this country—and see what it means to be a Young Socialist in that framework.

You also made the point that the Stalinists at the opening of the 1960s were still strong enough to aid the Cuban Revolution, but not strong enough to assassinate its revolutionary leadership. Can you expand on what happened afterwards in world politics that led to the disintegration of the Stalinist movement just a few decades later?

Part of a broader working-class vanguard

JACK BARNES: When someone joins the Young Socialists, they still need time to be able to understand, practically and concretely, what the party is. Joining the party is not a condition for being an active member of the Young Socialists. But it's only through coming to understand the party and what we're doing politically that a YS member really finds out what the communist movement is all about.

The Socialist Workers Party is not the leadership-in-becoming of the American socialist revolution. We're not an embryo that will grow in some direct way through recruitment into the party of the American socialist revolution. We're a conscious *political* vanguard, without which that leadership won't be put together. We're a nucleus of worker-bolsheviks who submit to the discipline of a revolutionary centralist proletarian party. But we're always seeking out and becoming part of a much broader vanguard of workers and farmers that is forming in the course of various struggles and leading *in action*. As future battles unfold, we will politically fuse more than once with other vanguard forces among workers and farmers who are coming from different origins and are forged by different experiences. The leadership of the coming American revolution will emerge out of that combined process; that's how any mass communist movement develops.

We don't tell new members they are joining what will

be the leadership of the future. We offer them the opportunity to join in the organized effort *today* to find, to work with, to learn from, and to influence this constantly changing and developing vanguard of the working class. To become part of a movement of proletarian cadres who are self-acting and self-willed—who fight by any means necessary to make the American socialist revolution, and struggle to win every possible demand to defend the interests of workers and the oppressed along the way.

Nobody has to look in a mirror and say: "I'm joining the leadership of the proletarian revolution." No, you're joining a politically conscious section, a political vanguard, of that emerging leadership, along the lines of the passages from *The Communist Manifesto* and *What Is To Be Done?* we talked about earlier today. That's much less of a burden!

IF THE RUSSIAN REVOLUTION and other victorious revolutions over the past century are any guide, then this vanguard will be much larger and much more heterogeneous than the party at every stage of the class struggle, right up through the insurrection itself. At important turning points, this broader proletarian vanguard will sometimes leapfrog the party, it will jump ahead of us, and our cadres will have to make the necessary adjustments and integrate ourselves more fully into the movement as it is developing in practice. That kind of tactical flexibility can only be shown in action by a party of worker-bolsheviks that is steeled in program and theory, confident in its strategic course, and organized on a revolutionary-centralist foundation. That's the kind of party whose cadres will win the loyalty and trust of growing numbers of vanguard workers and farmers, as we fight alongside each other and draw lessons together. That's the nucleus of the communist movement we're recruiting to today.

Don't forget. Workers in struggle decide who their leaders are. And that *is* who they are. Period. The party does not decide; that's one responsibility a worker-bolshevik does *not* have. And workers make the decision on who their leaders are based on what individuals do in struggle—not what party, union, church, or anything else they belong to.

Over the course of our political lives, each time we go back to books by Marx or Engels, Lenin or Trotsky, Cannon or Dobbs, we bring with us new developments in world politics and new experiences we're going through with other working people, as well as with newer generations in the party. It's not that our previous reading was less accurate or less valuable, but particular political lessons become more concrete because of what we're doing. We're rediscovering the importance of educational weekends and socialist summer schools where party and YS members work together, reading material before classes, studying, learning and relearning the history, strategy, and theory of the communist movement. Young Socialists are finding out how important it is to participate in the weekly Militant Labor Forums, where we discuss and debate politics together with other working people and youth attracted to these public meetings.

When we begin organizing a program of Marxist education today, always imagine that new members are saying: "No jargon, please!" When we have to put some ideas in normal language, experienced comrades often discover that we don't know everything we thought we knew. And we work on it together and learn it. If we can't communicate our politics broadly, so they can be understood, we can develop the illusion of knowledge rather than the real thing. We can start using the empty "group talk" of ingrown organizations.

Our educational work today brings together the older generations that came into our movement as Trotskyists with the generations that never will be Trotskyists. My generation and those who came before me were Trotskyists, as was the generation that followed mine. Without Trotsky and Trotskyism, the communist movement would not have survived for long after the consolidation of the Stalinist-led bureaucratic caste in the Soviet Union in the latter half of the 1920s. That's a historical fact, not a hypothesis. There would have been no Socialist Workers Party. There would have been no struggle for a proletarian party, in the United States or anywhere else.

But none of the comrades joining now, none who've joined over the past fifteen years or so, are Trotskyists or ever will be. Look at the final page of "Their Trotsky and Ours: Communist Continuity Today." It was originally a public talk given during a Young Socialist Alliance convention in Chicago at the end of 1982. "Most of us will not call our movement 'Trotskyist' before the decade is out, just as Trotsky never did," I said. "We in the Socialist Workers Party, like Trotsky, are communists."[46]

That's in fact what has happened. We are communists, pure and simple, worker-bolsheviks. Leaders of our movement who are working to organize the upcoming World Festival of Youth in Algiers are considered communists by most of those we collaborate with in that effort, as well as by those participants curious about the books and pam-

---

46. First published in 1983 in issue no. 1 of *New International*, "Their Trotsky and Ours" was subsequently reissued as a book: Jack Barnes, *Their Trotsky and Ours* (New York: Pathfinder, 2002). The passage referred to here appears on p. 147 [2008 printing].

phlets we bring to every international gathering. We're where you go to get communist literature. But I and others in my generation joined our movement and were trained and educated as Trotskyists. I'm glad we were, just as I'm proud that the same generations that pioneered the party's turn to industry, and the rebuilding of our industrial trade union fractions at the end of the 1970s, also initiated and led the deep-going effort through which we began identifying ourselves as what we are: communists. In the process, our Trotskyism per se was absorbed and withered away. This is what Trotsky fought for; what Jim Cannon fought for; what Farrell Dobbs and Joe Hansen fought for; what our movement has fought for since its origins here in the United States—to ensure the continuity, in theory and practice, of Bolshevism, of communism.

"We have no new revelation," Cannon said in the opening minutes of the talks that became *The History of American Trotskyism: 1928–38.* "Trotskyism is not a new movement, a new doctrine, but the restoration, the revival, of genuine Marxism as it was expounded and practiced in the Russian Revolution and in the early days of the Communist International."[47]

TROTSKY WROTE a wonderful article in 1937, entitled "Stalinism and Bolshevism," that I mentioned in the talk this morning. "Marxism found its highest historical expression in Bolshevism. Under the banner of Bolshevism the first victory of the proletariat was achieved and the first workers' state established," Trotsky said. The Bolshevik Party "was able to carry on its magnificent 'practical'

---

47. James P. Cannon, *The History of American Trotskyism*, p. 25 [2011 printing].

work only because it illuminated all its steps with theory. Bolshevism did not create this theory: it was furnished by Marxism." And as new developments unfolded in history, the Bolsheviks enriched that theory on the basis of their activity and generalizations from it.

"Bolshevism brought an invaluable contribution to Marxism," Trotsky said, "in its analysis of the imperialist epoch as an epoch of wars and revolutions; of bourgeois democracy in the era of decaying capitalism; of the correlation between the general strike and the insurrection; of the role of the party, soviets and trade unions in the period of proletarian revolution; in its theory of the Soviet state, of the economy of transition, of fascism and Bonapartism in the epoch of capitalist decline; finally in its analysis of the degeneration of the Bolshevik Party itself and of the Soviet state. Let any other tendency be named that has added anything essential to the conclusions and generalizations of Bolshevism."[48]

THE STALINISTS sought to claim the mantle of Bolshevism, with diminishing success over the decades. Just as they sought, as Joe Hansen once put it, to bask in "the red glow" of the Cuban Revolution in return for Moscow's military and economic assistance. The Cuban government's initiative in requesting that aid, and the speed of the Soviet response, were decisive to the survival of the revolution. This was true especially in the opening years, when Washington first imposed its economic embargo and still hoped to crush the revolution relatively rapidly through an invasion. In our resolutions and in our press,

48. Trotsky, "Stalinism and Bolshevism," *Trotsky Writings (1936–37)*, pp. 532, 548.

from that time to this, we have supported the decision of Fidel, Che, and other Cuban leaders to seek that assistance to defend and advance not only revolutionary Cuba but also the worldwide struggle for national liberation and socialism. But the Cuban leadership was, at the same time, always determined to limit their dependence on the Soviet Union—economically, militarily, and politically. They never forgot the lesson they learned during the October Crisis in 1962, when Premier Nikita Khrushchev didn't even consult them before ordering the Soviet missiles withdrawn from Cuba.

This begins to answer your second question, but it's necessary to emphasize a very important point: it was the *Soviet workers state* that was still strong enough to provide assistance to Cuba in those early years of the revolution, while it was *the world Stalinist movement* that had become too weak to successfully organize the murder of the central leadership in Cuba. The two are not the same thing: the Stalinist movement, organized to defend the interests of the caste in the Soviet Union, was the greatest source of the *weakening* of the conquests of the October Revolution. It was the Stalinist apparatus that cracked and disintegrated in 1990–91. A dozen years later the imperialists have still been unable to deal the kind of bloody defeat to the working class there that will be necessary in order to reimpose the dominance and stability of capitalist social relations in Russia and other republics of the former Soviet Union.

Initial signs of the disintegration of the world Stalinist movement were already well behind us by the 1960s, but they still used Marxist terminology and published large quantities not only of the classics of Marx, Engels, and Lenin but of their own propaganda and their own turgid manuals—what Che dubbed "the bricks." The shedding of the pretense to Marxism could come only from within the Soviet Union itself, and the decisive turning point came at the opening of the 1990s with what Fidel referred to as "the collapse of the meringue." After that it quickly ceased being possible for anyone to look to some apparatus in Moscow for even a counterfeit version of Marxism, much less the real thing.

Stalinism suffered a historic blow that sharply accelerated its decline. And soon, in historical terms, we will witness its disappearance. But our prognosis, the prognosis of the communist movement, going all the way back to the mid-1930s, has been confirmed: the bureaucratic caste proved to be weaker than the workers state itself, and Stalin*ism* as an ideology or a current within the working-class movement has no historical continuity, no foundation on which to perpetuate itself independent of the existence of that caste.

The real question about the semicolonial countries on the minds of many centrist forces, petty-bourgeois radicals, and other faint-hearts of various kinds since the early 1990s is this: without the prospect of aid from the Soviet Union, is it possible—or even politically responsible, some might say—for workers and peasants anywhere to make a revolution and bring to power a government that's intransigently anti-imperialist, let alone socialist? Is socialist revolution in this sense any longer even conceivable? If such a revolution were somehow to hold off or survive the political and military onslaught of the imperialist powers, especially Washington, wouldn't it be starved into submission? Of course, the bottom line is always this: "We've got to come to an accommodation with 'progressive' sections of our own bourgeoisie and of the two governing parties in the United States. We've got to move slowly and carefully. Above all, under these new conditions, we can't challenge the state power, the property, and the prerogatives of capital."

Some of these class-collaborationist political forces point to the defeat of the Nicaraguan revolution as the clincher. We've answered that argument, too. An entire issue of *New International* is devoted to explaining the powerful victory of the Nicaraguan workers and farmers government in 1979 and the reasons why the political leadership of the Sandinista National Liberation Front (FSLN) broke and retreated from a revolutionary internationalist course.[49]

WE SHOULD ALWAYS REMEMBER one thing: the Bolshevik-led workers and peasants of Russia had no other state power to turn to when they made a socialist revolution in October 1917. They turned the only direction they could: to the workers and farmers of Europe, Asia, and the world. They turned to the oppressed and exploited of the imperialist-dominated world. Their new Soviet government pursued a proletarian internationalist foreign policy. They reached out to revolutionary-minded toilers in every country they could to launch the Communist International. They offered their example and their aid. They reached more deeply among the popular masses of Soviet Russia itself. They built the Red Army and defended the workers and peasants republic against landlord-capitalist counterrevolution and imperialist invasion. And they took advantage of divisions among the imperialist powers and other capitalist governments that could buy them some time and breathing space—with-

---

49. See *New International* no. 9 (1994), "The Rise and Fall of the Nicaraguan Revolution."

out ever misleading workers, farmers, and revolutionary-minded youth who looked to the Bolsheviks about the irreformable character of these bourgeois regimes and the necessity to organize to overthrow each and every one of them.

That's what any victorious workers and peasants government anywhere in the world will set out to do again. They'll start with one bonus that the Bolsheviks did not have: revolutionary Cuba and its leadership, a leadership that has never refused to help a genuine revolution. Revolutionists today will fight in a world in which the working class is many times larger on every continent than it was in 1917. A world in which women have joined the battalions of the struggle for national liberation and socialism to a degree inconceivable eighty years ago. A world in which the direct colonial empires of finance capital have been vastly reduced. A world in which the imperialist system itself is wracked with its own accelerating conflicts and deepening contradictions and crises. A world where leaders from countries of every size, at every level of economic development, and from every oppressed national grouping have shown world-class ability as proletarian revolutionists—Thomas Sankara in Burkina Faso, Maurice Bishop in Grenada, and Malcolm X here in the United States are such examples. And militants can read what these revolutionary leaders said and what they did—in their own words—thanks to our decades-long communist publishing program, which is possible only because of the efforts of workers like you.

TODAY THERE IS NO prerevolutionary situation in any country in any part of the world where emulating the course of the Bolsheviks or the Cuban vanguard toward the seizure of power and establishment of a workers and farmers government is posed as an immediate concrete, practical task. That's not the point. The point is that without a clear perspective of the necessity of such a course, and the intransigent pursuit of it, no revolutionary party of the vanguard of workers and farmers can be educated, organized, and steeled as worker-bolsheviks today. And when wars, capitalist breakdowns, and social crises abruptly and unexpectedly give rise to revolutionary opportunities—as they will, over and over—it will be too late.

We don't guarantee a revolution will never fail. No. But we know that each proletarian revolution, even if it is defeated, helps prepare the next one—*if* an honest record and accurate lessons have been drawn by the communist vanguard and made available to coming generations. That has been true from the Paris Commune of 1871 to today. The question is never: How long can a victorious revolution hold out? Victorious revolutions don't "hold out." They don't "hang on." They aren't "preserved," like strawberries or apricots. Victorious revolutions set forces in motion. They reverberate far beyond their own borders. They educate and encourage workers and farmers in other countries fighting against exploitation and oppression. They galvanize solidarity among youth and working people within the imperialist centers. All of modern history teaches us this.

What's more, the economic and social conditions in which revolutions gestate and occur inevitably coincide with and provoke further crises and divisions among the imperialist powers themselves—and will do so increasingly in the years ahead. *Capitalism's World Disorder* remains just as timely a title as when we published the book two years ago, and will become more so.

Amid all these controlled and uncontrolled forces, it will be the courage, determination, solidarity, and class consciousness of the toilers—and the political preparation, combat experience, discipline, and timeliness of a communist leadership—that will be decisive. Not assistance from some outside force. And every step forward will be offered as an example and will make it more possible for revolutionaries anywhere in the world to move forward themselves.

THE TEAMSTER STRUGGLE

Teamster Rebellion
Teamster Power
Farrell Dobbs

Farrell Dobbs, a young worker who became part of the class-struggle leadership of the Minneapolis Teamsters in the 1930s, tells the story of the strikes and organizing drives that forged the industrial union movement throughout the Midwest of the United States. The first two of a series of four volumes written by a central leader of these battles and the communist movement. $19 each. Also in Spanish, French, and Swedish.

Teamster Politics

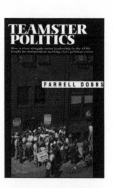

How the Minneapolis Teamsters combated FBI frame-ups, helped the jobless organize, deployed a Union Defense Guard to turn back fascist thugs, fought to advance independent labor political action, and mobilized opposition to US imperialism's entry into World War II. $19

Teamster Bureaucracy

How the employing class, backed by union bureaucrats, stepped up government efforts to gag class-conscious militants; how workers mounted a world campaign to free eighteen union and socialist leaders framed up and imprisoned in the infamous 1941 federal sedition trial. $19

Imperialism's March toward Fascism and War
Jack Barnes

"There will be new Hitlers, new Mussolinis. That is inevitable. What is not inevitable is that they will triumph. The working-class vanguard will organize our class to fight back against the devastating toll we are made to pay for the capitalist crisis. The future of humanity will be decided in the contest between these contending class forces." In *New International* no. 10. $16. Also in Spanish, French, Icelandic, and Swedish.

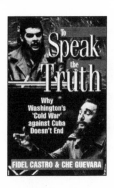

To Speak the Truth
Why Washington's 'Cold War' against Cuba Doesn't End
Fidel Castro, Ernesto Che Guevara

In historic speeches before the United Nations and UN bodies, Guevara and Castro address the peoples of the world, explaining why the US government so fears the example set by the socialist revolution in Cuba and why Washington's effort to destroy it will fail. $18

By Any Means Necessary
Malcolm X

"The imperialists know the only way you will voluntarily turn to the fox is to show you a wolf." In eleven speeches and interviews, Malcolm X presents a revolutionary alternative to this reformist trap, taking up political alliances, women's rights, US intervention in the Congo and Vietnam, capitalism and socialism, and more. $16

Capitalism's World Disorder
Working-Class Politics at the Millennium
Jack Barnes

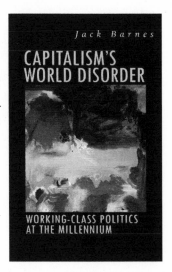

The social devastation and financial panic, the coarsening of politics, the cop brutality and acts of imperialist aggression accelerating around us—all are the product not of something gone wrong with capitalism but of its lawful workings. Yet the future can be changed by the united struggle and selfless action of workers and farmers conscious of their power to transform the world. $25. Also in Spanish and French.

Imperialism, the Highest Stage of Capitalism
V.I. Lenin

Imperialism not only increases the weight of debt bondage and parasitism in capitalist social relations, writes Lenin, but above all makes the competition of rival capitals—domestic and foreign—more violent and explosive. Amid capitalism's growing world disorder today, Lenin's 1916 booklet remains a foundation stone of the communist movement's program and activity. $10. Also in Spanish.

Europe and America
Two Speeches on Imperialism
Leon Trotsky

Writing in the mid-1920s, Bolshevik leader Leon Trotsky explains the emergence of the United States as imperialism's dominant economic and financial power following World War I. He describes the sharpening conflicts between Washington and its European rivals and highlights the revolutionary openings for the working class that would be played out in the decade to come. $12

Fascism: What It Is and How to Fight It
Leon Trotsky

Writing in the heat of struggle against the rise of fascism in Germany, France, and Spain in the 1930s, communist leader Leon Trotsky examines the class origins and character of fascist movements. Building on foundations laid by the Communist International in Lenin's time, Trotsky advances a working-class strategy to combat and defeat this malignant danger. $7

FARMING, SCIENCE,
AND THE WORKING CLASSES

The following article originally appeared as a four-part series in August 2001 in the socialist newsweekly the *Militant*, published in New York. It is edited and produced here as a single article. Steve Clark is the managing editor of *New International* and a member of the National Committee of the Socialist Workers Party.

The series, published under the title "Communism and Labor's Transformation of Nature," was written in response to a letter to the *Militant*'s editor from Karl Butts, a Florida farmer. It was based on a class by Clark presented at a June 2001 international socialist conference at Oberlin College in Ohio. Reprinted by permission of the *Militant*.

FARMING, SCIENCE,

AND THE WORKING CLASSES

by Steve Clark

A LETTER TO THE EDITOR from Karl Butts makes a good point concerning the final paragraph of an article by correspondent Joel Britton in the July 2 issue of the *Militant*. Britton paraphrased an interview with the director of an urban vegetable-growing cooperative in Havana, who explained that as in other large urban gardens they "began using substitutes for chemical pesticides and fertilizers by necessity during the Special Period, but now it is by choice."

Butts is right in saying that "by reporting this particular statement" at the conclusion of the article, the socialist press can seem to be giving "a certain political weight to the concept of organic production being preferable to that where 'chemicals' are used"—a view that is neither the editorial position of the *Militant* nor, I believe, the opinion of the author of that article. What's more, Butts points out, readers "may also come away thinking Cuba generally chooses not to use chemicals in agricultural production."

Britton visited Cuba in May as a *Militant* correspondent to cover the fortieth anniversary events of the National

Letter to the *Militant*

I read the article by Joel Britton in your July 2 [2001] issue headlined, "Cubans celebrate 40th anniversary of farmers organization." As a small farmer who recently participated in a Cuba-U.S. farmer-to-farmer tour, guests of the National Association of Small Farmers of Cuba (ANAP), I found the article a good summary of what Cuban farmers have accomplished over the past four decades as a result of their socialist revolution and land reform. The description of how the revolution organized to overcome the food shortages of the worst years of the economic crisis of the early 1990s—what Cubans call the Special Period—was also useful.

I was concerned, however, about the last paragraph of the article, where Britton quotes the director of one of Havana's urban gardens. The article says that the director explained "that as in other large urban gardens they began using substitutes for chemical pesticides and fertilizers by necessity during the Special Period, but now it is by choice."

My understanding is that the urban garden program was instituted in 1994 as one of the measures aimed at making food more accessible to workers in urban areas. The law setting up the program stipulated certain chemicals and fertilizers would be prohibited out of concern for people living and working in close proximity to the farms. So a choice never existed, if this is true. This would be only a quibble, if it weren't for the impression readers of the *Militant* might take away in reading this paragraph that the socialist press, by reporting this particular statement, has given a certain political weight to the concept of organic production being preferable to that where "chemicals" are used. At least this is how it struck me. Readers may also come away thinking Cuba generally chooses not to use chemicals in agricultural production.

Organic farming is a bourgeois concept, and it has nothing to do with the fight to feed the world. I don't think it is in the interests of workers and farmers to give any credence to this marketing ploy in the socialist press. Communists in imperialist countries should be especially sensitive about being perceived as advocating idealistic solutions in a world with 800 million chronically hungry.

Karl Butts
Tampa, Florida

Association of Small Farmers (ANAP). Together with Wisconsin dairy farmer Randy Jasper and Carolyn Lane of Minnesota, a member of Food First, Britton also participated in the May 17–19 Fourth International Meeting on Organic Agriculture, sponsored by the Cuban Association of Agricultural and Forestry Technicians.

Cuba's achievements

As Britton explained in the article, "Many of the presentations at the conference centered on how Cuban farmers, supported by the country's revolutionary leadership, responded in the early 1990s to a sharp drop in the availability of chemical fertilizers, herbicides, and pesticides, as well as fuel and parts needed to keep machinery running. Workers and farmers turned decisively to the use of substitutes for fertilizers and pesticides. For example, they began using bagasse, a residue of sugar production, as fertilizer."

Prior to 1990, trade with the Soviet Union as well as with other countries in the Council of Mutual Economic Assistance, much of it on favorable terms, had accounted for 81 percent of Cuba's foreign trade. With the collapse of the Stalinist regimes in Central and Eastern Europe and the USSR, Cuba no longer had any buffer against the shocks of the world capitalist market. At the same time, both Democratic and Republican administrations intensified Washington's economic warfare against Cuba as well.

During the most difficult years of that crisis in the opening half of the 1990s, for example, farm-related consumption of diesel fuel and other petroleum-based energy sources was cut in half in Cuba—forcing farmers to idle tractors and other machinery and return to the widespread use of oxen in the fields. The application of chemical fertilizers, herbicides, and pesticides dropped by 80 percent. Imports of wheat and other grains fell by 50 percent, and the drop-off in many other imported food products was even steeper.

One important way the revolutionary government responded to the resulting food shortages was through organizing working people to establish urban vegetable gardens, often set up as cooperatives. This growing urban agricultural workforce provides fresh produce to schools, hospitals, and workplace cafeterias. The cooperatives also sell directly to the public and help supply a network of markets in Havana and other cities. During the trip, Britton and other conference participants visited three such small-scale farms in the Havana area organized as Basic Units of Cooperative Production (UBPCs). More than 50 percent of Havana's fresh produce is now provided by the some sixty thousand Cubans working in urban agriculture.[1] Given the large concentrations of people living around the gardens, the Cuban government, as Butts points out in his letter, prohibits the use of chemical fertilizers or pesticides within city limits.

In face of sharply reduced imports, and spurred on by national health policies, the Cuban government over the past decade has educated and organized farmers and workers to substitute organic for chemical inputs in much

---

1. In 2003 workers engaged in small-scale farming in and around Cuban cities produced 3.9 million tons of vegetables and herbs, up from 4,600 tons in 1994. In addition, 250,000 tons of rice were produced on small-scale plots. Some 350,000 Cubans now work in small-scale, predominantly urban food cultivation, almost as many as the 420,000 employed in large-scale agriculture in rural areas.

of agricultural production. Centers have been established across the island where workers produce enriched compost and rock phosphates to replace manufactured chemical fertilizers. Pesticides and herbicides produced using bacteria and fungi, together with natural predators, are being used to control pests. Under the brand name Biasav, Cuba has begun marketing a line of its biological pesticides and herbicides around the world. Some of the methods farmers are using today in Cuba have long-term benefits for the soil, the water, and the health of human beings and other creatures, while also making it possible for farmers to improve crop yields.

No 'Golden Age'

As Butts points out, however, it is simply false that "Cuba generally chooses not to use chemicals in agricultural production." Synthetic fertilizers, pesticides, and herbicides are used in the production of sugar, which has historically been Cuba's main export crop, as well as in the cultivation of rice, coffee, tobacco, potatoes, and many other commodities. Moreover, as improved economic conditions enable them to do so, the Cuban government and people will undoubtedly choose once again to increase the use of such chemical farm inputs and technologies as are relatively safe, if doing so helps farmers and farmworkers increase productivity, reduce backbreaking labor, and feed and clothe more people at lower cost.

In the name of protecting the environment, and sometimes in the name of defending the Cuban Revolution as well, some organizations and individuals turn the measures Cubans have been forced to take under crisis conditions into a return to some kind of idyllic Golden Age. An example is a February 2001 article by the CEO of the Vermont-based Gardener's Supply Company. "Cuba leads the developing world," he writes, "in small-scale composting, organic soil reclamation, irrigation and crop rotation research, animal powered traction (oxen) and other innovative practices."

To be sure, Cuba does lead the semicolonial world. The accomplishments of Cuban workers and farmers during and after the Special Period offer striking confirmation of their commitment to the socialist revolution. What they achieved in face of the extremely difficult economic and social conditions of the 1990s would have been inconceivable in any other country in the world today.

But lumping in a return by farmers to the use of animal traction—without qualification—is a different matter. While the harnessing of oxen to plow fields was an "innovative practice" in humanity's Neolithic Period six thousand years ago, few Cuban toilers would call its widespread use today anything but a dire necessity, one they intend to put behind them as soon as conditions allow.

What does 'organic' mean?

The issues raised by Butts are broader than the agricultural policies of the Cuban Revolution over the past decade. They pose one of the most fundamental questions of communist theory and practice: the transformation of nature by social labor, without which the fight by the working class to put an end to exploitation and oppression is a utopian illusion.

Karl Marx, a founding leader of the modern revolutionary workers movement, wrote in *Capital*:

> Labor is, first of all, a process between man
> and nature, a process by which man, through his
> own actions, mediates, regulates and controls

the metabolism between himself and nature. He confronts the materials of nature as a force of nature. He sets in motion the natural forces which belong to his own body, his arms, legs, head and hands, in order to appropriate the materials of nature in a form adapted to his own needs. Through this movement he acts upon external nature and changes it, and in this way he simultaneously changes his own nature. He develops the potentialities slumbering within nature, and subjects the play of its forces to his own sovereign power.[2]

As Butts says, the notion that organic farming is somehow inherently superior to the use of synthetic inputs by farmers is false and contrary to the historic interests of the great toiling majority of humanity. When statements open to misinterpretation along these lines were made by a couple of participants in a national leadership meeting of the Socialist Workers Party in May 2001, SWP national secretary Jack Barnes addressed them in his summary report to the gathering.

"What has 'organic' come to mean to workers when used in reference to food?" Barnes asked. "It means 'more expensive'—that's what it means. All products of human labor under capitalism are turned into commodities. So, when you see something at the grocery store christened 'organic,' that means the U.S. Department of Agriculture has OK'd slapping a label on it enabling marketers to put a higher price tag on it too."

A decade ago so-called organic foods could be found

---

2. Karl Marx, *Capital*, vol. 1 (London: Penguin, 1986), p. 283. First published in German in 1867.

only in specialized "natural foods" shops catering to a small, largely middle-class market (price differentials were even greater back then). Today, however, virtually every food monopoly has bought up small businesses and launched its own product line. General Mills, Gerber, Dole, Heinz, ConAgra, Archer Daniels Midland—all have their own "organic" brand names, selling at a premium price to a growing niche market in grocery chains. (Revolutionary Cuba itself has been able to tap into this niche to offset at least a tiny portion of its losses from the declining price of sugar on the world capitalist market. Recently Cuba has begun cultivating a small quantity of sugar using only biological inputs that it sells—well above standard commodity prices—to European chocolatiers and specialties purveyors of packaged organic brown sugar.)

From its origins in the mid-nineteenth century, organic farming as "a cause"—as opposed to this or that particular method of cultivation—has been associated with a suspicion of science and technology among layers of the middle class and bohemian bourgeois circles. Many of its champions in the opening five or six decades of the twentieth century were also affiliated to the political ultraright. They shared kinship with the right-wing conspiracy theorists of the 1950s and 1960s who campaigned to stop the fluoridation of water and toothpaste—an effort that has been revived in recent years with the backing of Ralph Nader and various other capitalist reformers labeling themselves "environmentalists."

How capitalism works

"When class-conscious workers and farmers speak of 'sustainable' agriculture," Barnes said at the SWP leadership meeting, "what we're aiming to sustain is the increasingly productive transformation of nature by social labor to meet humanity's needs."

Given the competition of capitals and imperatives of war-related research and development in the imperialist system, Barnes said, nothing is going to stop the application of science and new technologies to both industrial and agricultural production. At the same time, nothing is going to stop the allocation of capital to maximize the rulers' short-term extraction of surplus value. That is what drives capitalist production, not advancing human health, welfare, or long-term social goals of any kind. Since all commodities under capitalism are produced and marketed only with profits in mind—not their utility to human beings—all of them, "whether 'natural' or 'synthetic,' are subject to poisons, contamination, or shoddy workmanship," Barnes pointed out.

These political questions had been addressed by Barnes in a section of his 1999 book, *Capitalism's World Disorder: Working-Class Politics at the Millennium.* "True environmental horrors are accelerating under capitalism today (and the anti-working-class, Stalinist regimes across Central and Eastern Europe and the USSR are responsible for unthinkable devastation as well)," Barnes said. "Revolutionary governments of the workers and farmers can and will reverse this deadly course."[3]

Karl Marx and Frederick Engels wrote powerfully and convincingly about capital's destruction of the soil, the water, the air—the bases of human life and civilization. Even before they had fully developed their proletarian world outlook, Barnes pointed out, each of them as revolutionary-minded young people had been pro-

---

3. Jack Barnes, *Capitalism's World Disorder: Working-Class Politics at the Millennium* (New York: Pathfinder, 1999), p. 333 [2012 printing].

foundly affected by what they saw all around them—
whether in the newly industrializing German Rhineland
where they grew up, or during trips to Great Britain
where the factory system was the most advanced in the
world. They recognized the toll capitalism was taking
on the nutrition and sanitary conditions of the working
class and on the acceleration of the fouling of the natural environment.

As early as 1845, when Marx and Engels were both in
their twenties and still almost two years away from joining
a workers organization and helping draft its program, the
Communist Manifesto, they observed that in the development of capitalism "there comes a stage when productive forces . . . are brought into being which, under the
existing relations, only cause mischief and are no longer
productive but destructive forces."[4]

II

ADVANCING THE WORLDWIDE STRUGGLE for socialism necessitates closing the enormous gap in
economic, social, and cultural conditions among
working people of different countries, and toilers of city
and countryside. These inequitable conditions are inherited from millennia of class society and have been
reproduced by the imperialist world order over the last
century.

Roughly two billion people, for example, have no access either to electricity or to any but the most primitive

---

4. Marx and Engels, "The German Ideology," in Marx and Engels, *Collected Works*, vol. 5 (Moscow: Progress Publishers, 1986),
p. 52.

fuels for cooking and heating. Candles and kerosene for lighting, and wood, dung, thatch, and straw for fire (all with their noxious fumes, harmful both to humans and the earth's atmosphere) are the reality for at least one-third of the world's population. Some 57 percent of the world's electricity is consumed in the imperialist countries of North America, Europe, and the Pacific, which have 14 percent of the earth's population. Only 10 percent of the electricity, on the other hand, is consumed in Asia and the Pacific (excluding Japan and China), which have 31 percent of the world's population. And 1 percent is consumed in sub-Saharan Africa, with nearly 10 percent of the world's population.

Another indication of this global inequity perpetrated by the world capitalist system can be seen in the varying application of farming techniques that help tillers increase their productivity. While in the imperialist countries there are sixteen tractors in use by farmers for every one thousand acres of land, there are only three in use on average elsewhere in the world. And with the exception of the rice-producing semicolonial countries of East Asia, farmers' application of fertilizer per acre is much higher in North America, Europe, Australia, New Zealand, and Japan.

This imperialist-imposed backwardness in agriculture and industry has devastating effects on the economic, social, and cultural conditions and development of working people in Asia, Africa, and Latin America. According to even the understated estimates of finance capital's international agencies, some 47 percent of the world's population—nearly half—subsist on less than $2 a day. Forty percent have no access to basic sanitation. Similar estimates count at least one billion adults as being illiterate worldwide—more than a quarter of all adults in the oppressed nations of Asia, Africa, and Latin America. This includes 60 percent of adults in sub-Saharan Africa and 55 percent in South Asia, with much higher rates for women not only in these regions but also in most of the rest of the world. And as Butts notes at the close of his letter, some eight hundred million people worldwide are estimated by the United Nations World Food Programme to be chronically hungry, with many more suffering from malnutrition.

Continuity with Bolshevism

The preconditions to advancing the struggle for socialism on a world scale today remain fundamentally the same as those presented eight decades ago by Bolshevik leader V.I. Lenin. In explaining the centrality of the effort to advance the industrialization of the young Soviet republic in February 1920, Lenin said:

> We must show the peasants that the organization of industry on the basis of modern, advanced technology, on electrification which will provide a link between town and country, will put an end to the division between town and country, will make it possible to raise the level of culture in the countryside and to overcome, even in the most remote corners of the land, backwardness, ignorance, poverty, disease, and barbarism.[5]

The construction of socialism, Lenin said in late December of that year, requires more than just literacy

5. V.I. Lenin, "Report on the Work of the All-Russia Central Executive Committee," Lenin, *Collected Works* (Moscow: Progress Publishers, 1965), vol. 30, p. 335. Hereafter *LCW.*

among the toilers engaged in that historic effort. "We need cultured, enlightened and educated working people," he said, so that not only urban workers but "the majority of the peasants [are] aware of the tasks awaiting us."[6]

Traditional methods?

Karl Butts is correct that the elevation of "organic" farming to a fetish does not begin from "the fight to feed the world." Those who would reject progress in agricultural chemistry and technology in favor of what advocates of organic farming sometimes call natural or traditional methods should recall three things:

First, life expectancy at birth in the earliest agricultural communities some ten thousand years ago was well under thirty years of age.

Second, as a result of scientific advances in plant breeding, fertilizers, pesticides, irrigation, and mechanization, world grain yields have doubled since 1960, while it took one thousand years in England for wheat yields to quadruple to their current level.

Third, there are few methods so destructive to the environment and inimical to sustainable food production as slash-and-burn agriculture and overgrazing, both typical of so-called traditional farming in much of the world. Farmers' use of relatively modern methods of crop rotation, as well as fertilizer and pesticides, both synthetic and natural, register enormous and "unnatural" progress in recent centuries for both human beings and the environment in which we live and labor.

The history of capitalist agriculture has been one that

6. Lenin, "Speech to the Eighth All-Russia Congress of Soviets," *LCW*, vol. 31, p. 518.

combines advances in the productivity of farm labor with the use of profit-maximizing methods that exhaust and erode the soil, pollute water sources, and poison farmers, workers, and consumers. Marx wrote about these questions at length in *Capital*, at a time when big advances in the knowledge of the chemistry of soil fertility were making it possible for farmers, through the application of synthetic fertilizers, to counteract the exhaustion of fields and substantially increase yields. Factory workers first produced "superphosphate" fertilizers in Britain in 1843, to be followed in Germany, France, and the United States over the next three decades.

MARX ANSWERED VARIOUS early bourgeois writers on farming who, "on account of the state of agricultural chemistry in their time" made the false claim that "there is a limit to the amount of capital which can be invested in a spatially limited field." To the contrary, Marx said in *Capital*, the earth "continuously improves, as long as it is treated correctly." In fact, agriculture has an advantage over factory production in this regard. New machinery depreciates with use, he pointed out, and investments in new industrial technology tend to make prior improvements obsolete. With the soil, however, "successive capital investments can have their benefit without the earlier ones being lost."[7]

At the same time, Marx recognized that the application of all scientific and technological advances under bourgeois social relations is subject to the competition of capitals to maximize profits. In the very next chapter of *Capital*, "The Genesis of Capitalist Ground-Rent," he

---

7. Marx, *Capital*, vol. 3 (London: Penguin, 1981), pp. 915–16.

pointed to the consequences of capital's growing domination of agriculture, which drives more and more farmers and their families into hopeless debt and then off the land. This process, Marx wrote, "reduces the agricultural population to an ever decreasing minimum and confronts it with an ever growing industrial population crammed together in large towns. . . . The result of this is a squandering of the vitality of the soil." Marx continued:

> Large-scale industry and industrially pursued large-scale agriculture have the same effect. If they are originally distinguished by the fact that the former lays waste and ruins labor-power and thus the natural power of man, whereas the latter does the same to the natural power of the soil, they link up in the later course of development, since the industrial system applied to agriculture also enervates the workers there, while industry and trade for their part provide agriculture with the means of exhausting the soil.[8]

In a section of *Capital* entitled, "Large-scale industry and agriculture," Marx wrote:

> A conscious, technological application of science replaces the previous highly irrational and slothfully traditional way of working. The capitalist mode of production completes the disintegration of the primitive familial union which bound agriculture and manufacture together when they were both at an undeveloped and childlike stage. But at the same time it creates the material

---

8. Marx, *Capital*, vol. 3, p. 950.

conditions for a new and higher synthesis, a union of agriculture and industry.

While capitalism "creates the material conditions" for such an advance, Marx continued, the propertied families' ruthless exploitation of both human beings and nature create an insuperable obstacle to this union and thus the progress of civilization. He wrote:

> In modern agriculture, as in urban industry, the increase in the productivity and the mobility of labor is purchased at the cost of laying waste and debilitating labor-power itself. Moreover, all progress in capitalist agriculture is a progress in the art, not only of robbing the worker, but of robbing the soil; all progress in increasing the fertility of the soil for a given time is a progress towards ruining the more long-lasting sources of that fertility. . . . Capitalist production, therefore, only develops the techniques and the degree of combination of the social process of production by simultaneously undermining the original sources of all wealth—the soil and the worker.[9]

Frederick Engels, Marx's lifelong collaborator in the leadership of the communist movement, also described this process in many of his writings, including the unfinished 1876 article, "The Part Played by Labor in the Transition from Ape to Man." Engels wrote:

> What cared the Spanish planters in Cuba who burned down forests on the slopes of the

---

9. Marx, *Capital*, vol. 1, pp. 637–38.

mountains and obtained from the ashes sufficient
fertilizer for one generation of highly profitable
coffee trees—what cared they that the heavy
tropical rainfall afterwards washed away the now-
unprotected upper stratum of the soil, leaving
behind only bare rock! In relation to nature, as
to society, the present mode of production is
predominantly concerned only about the first,
the most tangible result; and then surprise is
even expressed that the most remote effects of
actions directed to this end turn out to be of
quite a different, mainly even of quite an opposite,
character.[10]

Imperialism, the arsonist

Engels's example, drawn from the early years of capitalism in the eighteenth and early nineteenth centuries, remains an apt description of the rapacious and destructive
course of international finance capital to this day. It calls
to mind the 1986 speech on trees and forests presented
at an international conference in Paris by Thomas Sankara, leader of the 1983–87 popular revolutionary government of the West African country of Burkina Faso, a
former French colony.

Sankara described the "creeping desert" in Burkina
and a number of other countries at the northern edge
of sub-Saharan Africa. Exhaustion of the soil—which
advances month by month, year by year across the
continent—is contributing to the hunger, disease, and
economic and social devastation of millions. "I have

---

10. Published as an appendix to *The Origin of the Family, Private Property, and the State* (New York: Pathfinder, 1972), p. 275
[2010 printing].

come to join with you in deploring the harshness of nature," Sankara told the conference, whose participants included the president of France and other top figures in the imperialist government. "But I have also come to denounce the ones whose selfishness is the source of his fellow man's misfortune. Colonial plunder has decimated our forests without the slightest thought of replenishing them for our tomorrows." Sankara continued:

> The unpunished disruption of the biosphere by savage and murderous forays on the land and in the air continues. . . . Those who have the technological means to find the culprits have no interest in doing so, and those who have an interest in doing so lack the technological means. They have only their intuition and their innermost conviction.
>
> We are not against progress, but we do not want progress that is anarchic and criminally neglects the rights of others. We therefore wish to affirm that the battle against the encroachment of the desert is a battle to establish a balance between man, nature, and society. As such it is a political battle above all, and not an act of fate. . . .
>
> As Karl Marx said, those who live in a palace do not think about the same things, nor in the same way, as those who live in a hut. This struggle to defend the trees and forests is above all a struggle against imperialism. Because imperialism is the arsonist setting fire to our forests and our savannas.[11]

---

11. Thomas Sankara, *Thomas Sankara Speaks* (New York: Pathfinder, 1988, 2007), pp. 257–59 [2012 printing].

III

THE LATEST FOCUS of middle-class fear, anxiety, and ignorance in face of capital's disdain for life and nature is the near-hysterical campaign against foods cultivated from seeds that have undergone a transplant of a strand of genetic material, DNA, from a different plant species—so-called transgenic organisms, or Genetically Modified Organisms (GMOs).

Humanity has been modifying the genetic makeup of plants and animals ever since the dawn of agriculture and domestication. Otherwise there would be none of the cattle, pigs, horses, cats, and dogs we're familiar with today, nor the varieties of wheat, corn, rice, vegetables, cotton, and other produce we use for food and fiber. Those modifications, however, were the result of selective crossbreeding to produce new and desired varieties and traits. GMOs involve the actual transfer of genes from one species to another.

There was no outcry against this scientific procedure (and largely still isn't) when it was first applied to the production of insulin, needed by diabetics, in greater quantities and of higher quality than the previous procedure of extracting insulin from the pancreas of pigs and cows. There was little or no outcry in response to the development of a "biotech" vaccine to treat hepatitis B, as well as numerous other medicines over the past two decades. With the application of genetic engineering to agriculture over the past six years, however, there has been a growing uproar from various environmentalist groups and related protest organizations, as they have attracted bourgeois sponsors advancing their own propertied interests and a substantial middle-class following.

Since the manufacture of GMOs is dominated by giant U.S. agribusiness, and such seeds are most widely sown in

U.S. fields, the issue has also become a political football in the intensifying interimperialist competition for markets between Wall Street and Washington and its rivals in Europe and Asia. The United Kingdom's Prince Charles has become among the most prominent anti-GMO spokespeople in Europe. In a widely published speech in May 2000, His Royal Highness called for a rediscovery of "the essential unity and order of the living and spiritual world—as in the case of organic agriculture," as well as for the improvement of "traditional systems of agriculture, which have stood the all-important test of time."

(It seems fitting to recall that Her Royal Highness, the late Princess Diana, helped spearhead another international campaign serving the interests of the imperialist bourgeoisie, this one in support of an international treaty against the use of land mines. The Cuban government has refused to sign the pact, correctly pointing out that—in face of the much more massively armed imperialist governments that are pressing the treaty, and their never-ending wars of conquest—land mines remain "the weapons of the poor.")

Banners and posters demanding "Stop Frankenfoods!" have become a staple among the melange of protectionist, nationalist, and anti-big-business slogans raised by a spectrum of environmentalist reformers, trade union officials, farmers fearful of growing monopoly competition, as well as anarchists and other petty-bourgeois radical currents. Their cry has been heard outside meetings of imperialist associations such as the World Trade Organization, International Monetary Fund, and "G-8" governments—from Seattle to Prague, Melbourne, and Quebec; from Washington, D.C., to Davos, Gothenburg, and Genoa.

The main use so far of genetically modified seeds in

farming is to increase crop resistance to insects and weed-killing herbicides. The GMO seeds enable farmers to produce higher yields with less need for costly and toxic pesticides. Seeds are also being developed that reduce the need for tillage and resulting soil erosion, are more tolerant to drought, and germinate rice and other grains with enriched nutritional value.

Since the first planting for the market of genetically modified crops in the mid-1990s, GMO seeds have become available for corn, cotton, squash, potatoes, canola, soybeans, and sugar beets. More than a fifth of all corn in the United States is now grown in this manner, and the planting of GMO seeds for soybeans is substantially higher. There has been a twenty-fold increase worldwide in acreage planted with genetically modified seeds, almost all in the United States, Canada, and Argentina.[12]

No evidence of harm

Despite the shrill pitch of the campaigns against "genetic pollution," there is not a single documented case of a human being anywhere in the world being harmed by food or medicine because it is produced in this way. Nor is there a single example of dreaded armies of "superweeds" vanquishing fields and wetlands. By their very origins, in fact, genetically modified plants are particularly dependent on human care and cultivation; on their own, they

---

12. By 2003 global acreage of GMO crops had increased forty-fold since 1996—to 167 million acres under cultivation by seven million farmers in eighteen countries. In the United States, as of 2002, 75 percent of the soybean crop, 71 percent of the cotton, and 34 percent of corn were grown by farmers using GMO seeds. The other five countries in which the most acreage was sown with transgenic crops were Argentina, Canada, Brazil, China, and South Africa.

are poorly adapted to nature "red in tooth and claw."

The world view advanced by various advocates of the inherent superiority of "organic" agriculture is not neutral in its effects on the conditions and prospects for liberation of working people, either those in the oppressed nations of Asia, Africa, and Latin America or those in the imperialist countries. Environmentalist organizations, for example, waged a successful effort against the unquestionably toxic pesticide DDT, resulting in a welcome halt to its use throughout the imperialist world. No comparable energy or resources, however, are now being devoted to campaigning against various imperialist governments and agencies that are refusing to fund the use of DDT in some twenty-five semicolonial countries where—applied in relatively small quantities—it remains the most effective way to control mosquitoes that spread malaria. More than one million people each year die from that disease worldwide, most of them children. Some strains recur for a lifetime in those who are "cured."

Capitalism fouls things up

As with all creations of human labor, the products of science and technology are put to use by the capitalist exploiters in order to maximize individual profits, not to meet social needs. Without the independent political mobilization of labor and its allies to fight for political power, the employers, their governments, and their parties act with utter disregard for the consequences to human health, safety, and the natural environment.

Because "individual capitalists are engaged in production and exchange for the sake of immediate profits," wrote Engels in 1876, only "the most immediate results can be taken into account in the first place. As long as the individual manufacturer or merchant sells a manufactured or purchased commodity with the usual coveted profit, he is satisfied and does not concern himself with what afterwards becomes of the commodity and its purchasers."[13]

This is true whether that commodity is a Ford Explorer, Odwalla organic apple juice, a lump of A.T. Massey coal, a Boeing 757, a genetically modified soybean, or a hybrid ear of corn selectively crossbred a century or more ago. In all these cases, the health and safety of workers, farmers, and the broader public alike are sacrificed on the altar of profits with light "inspection" and "regulation" by agencies of a government that represents the class interests of capital.

The 'seed police'

The biggest social issue raised by the advent of GMO seeds is the one least often pointed to either in the big-business press or by most opponents of genetic modification. This innovation is used by capitalist trusts such as Monsanto, Pioneer, Dow, and others to intensify the exploitation of working farmers.

In face of competition from capitalist farmers, small producers cannot afford to forego new methods and technologies that reduce their hours (and burdens) of labor and decrease materials costs. A working farmer who wants to continue tilling the land or raising livestock does not have the option of relying on horses rather than tractors, of not using a modern harvester or combine, of doing without fertilizer and pesticides, or of sowing seed with low yields. That's why more and more farmers in the United States are using genetically modified seed. But

---

13. Engels, "The Part Played by Labor in the Transition from Ape to Man," in *The Origin of the Family, Private Property, and the State*, p. 275.

they pay a substantial social price in doing so. In order to purchase the seed, they are forced to enter into legally binding agreements with Monsanto, Pioneer, and other monopolies that they will not use the seed produced by the crop to sow their next planting and will not sell that seed to other farmers. The farmer is contractually bound to return to the same company the next year to buy more patented seed if they want to plant the crop again.

Giant corporations such as Monsanto send inspectors—the "seed police"—to take clippings from farmers' crops to enforce these contracts. Monsanto has placed ads in farm journals warning that anyone who violates these terms is "committing an act of piracy [that] could cost a farmer hundreds of dollars per acre in cash settlements and legal fees, plus multiple years of on-farm and business records inspection." By 1998 Monsanto announced it had already filed 475 "seed piracy" suits nationwide, and was actively pursuing 250 more based on some 1,800 "leads" in twenty U.S. states. The company had won judgments in the United States ranging from $10,000 to $35,000, driving already deeply indebted farmers closer to insolvency and bank foreclosure on their land. In Canada, as of mid-1999 Monsanto had settled eight such cases out of court and was pursuing others. The grain giant won a lawsuit against a canola farmer in Saskatchewan whose crop was found to have plants grown from seed blown by the wind from a neighboring field.[14]

The agribusiness monopolists are also patenting

---

14. In May 2004 Canada's Supreme Court upheld Monsanto's case against the farmer but denied damages to the company. In the United States, as of early 2004, some one hundred suits filed by Monsanto had gone to trial, with courts awarding the company damages averaging $100,000 for each farmer.

plants whose seeds are unable to germinate—a harvest of mules!

Laws of the market system

These consequences of the purchase of genetically modified seeds from capitalist suppliers is not unique. It is one of myriad ways working farmers are squeezed between the rising costs of inputs they must purchase from the owners of one set of capitalist trusts, and the downward pressure on prices they receive for their grain, livestock, milk, and other produce from other monopolies.

This is another outcome of the laws of the capitalist market system that increasingly foster the spread of so-called "contract farming," which, especially in the imperialist centers, ties farmers who produce hogs, poultry, cattle, and a variety of vegetables to corporations that dictate every aspect of their procedures and to whom they are bound to sell their output at set prices. In short, the spread of GMO seeds is one more factor accelerating capital's relentless proletarianization of layer after layer of working farmers—in North America and worldwide.

But it is no more in the interests of working farmers and their allies in the ranks of labor to oppose advances in the science of agriculture than it was for workers in the early nineteenth century to oppose the introduction of the power loom and other machinery. "If machinery is the most powerful means of raising the productivity of labor, i.e., of shortening the working time needed to produce a commodity," Marx wrote in *Capital*, "it is also, as a repository of capital, the most powerful means of lengthening the working day beyond all natural limits in those industries first directly seized on by it."[15]

---

15. Marx, *Capital*, vol. 1, p. 526.

Not only did these new "labor-saving" devices enable capitalists to extend the hours of labor, intensify speedup, and throw employed workers onto the streets, Marx pointed out, but factory work, "at the same time, does away with the many-sided play of the muscles, and confiscates every atom of freedom, both in bodily and intellectual activity. Even the lightening of the labor becomes an instrument of torture, since the machine does not free the workers from the work, but rather deprives the work itself of all content."[16] That's why, Marx explained, some workers in the early 1800s organized what became known as the Luddite movement and stormed through workshops destroying the newly introduced machines.

"It took both time and experience before the workers learnt to distinguish between machinery and its employment by capital," Marx wrote, "and therefore to transfer their attacks from the material instruments of production to the form of society which utilizes those instruments."[17] It continues to require time and experience and proletarian leadership.

IV

THE U.S. RULERS are not only global capitalism's leading bankers and manufacturers. U.S. capitalism also leads the imperialist world in both agricultural output and exports. Nationalist voices of the U.S. bourgeoisie, from capitalist farmers to grain monopolies and government agencies, trumpet the "miracle of American farming."

16. Ibid., p. 548.

17. Ibid., pp. 554–55.

"American farmers grow food that helps feed the world," says the U.S. Department of Agriculture (USDA).

"America's farmers and ranchers are equipped to feed the world in the 21st century," says the president of the capitalist-dominated Farm Bureau Federation.

"Our mission is to feed and nourish a growing world population," says the Web site of the grain giant Archer Daniels Midland. And its top competitor, Cargill, speaks of "helping farmers grow a wide variety of goods to feed a growing world."

The American Soybean Association recently organized a campaign of postcards to the USDA built around the slogan, "America's Surplus Soybeans Can Feed a Hungry World."

The first thing to note about these chauvinist claims is that they are simply lies. "America"—that classless fiction behind which a handful of U.S. propertied families shield their domination of the armed forces, cops, courts, and other institutions of the capitalist state based in Washington—does not feed the world. In 1998, for example, the twenty-five countries cited by the United Nations Food and Agriculture Organization as having the world's greatest levels of undernourishment received less than 0.03 percent of U.S. soybean exports, and in 1996 they received none! They were the destination of less than 0.3 percent of U.S. corn exports in 1996, as well.

What does "feeding the world" mean, anyway, when according to United Nations figures nearly 50 percent of children under age five in South Asia are underweight? Nearly one-third in sub-Saharan Africa? More than 15 percent in the Middle East and East Asia and the Pacific? Nearly 10 percent in Latin America and the Caribbean? What does it mean when right in the United States itself, according to the U.S. Department of Agriculture, some ten million people are estimated to be hungry, and another twenty-one million go for parts of each year without "enough food for an active, healthy life"?

Nor are working farmers faring well under the laws of motion of capital in the United States and worldwide. According to a study released in June 2001, some thirty-three thousand U.S. farms have gone under since the early 1990s. Prices paid to Mexican corn farmers fell by half over that period, driving many more off the land there. While farmers in Canada suffered a 20 percent drop in their net incomes between 1989 and 1999.

The monopolies that dominate U.S. and world food markets, however, have done much better. Between the mid-1970s and the dawn of the twenty-first century, for example, food prices paid by consumers in the United States shot up by 250 percent, while the prices received by farmers in real terms over that period have stagnated at best. No wonder the latest annual figures show Archer Daniels Midland posting more than $300 million in after-tax profits, while ConAgra raked in $683 million.[18]

Cuba's example

Contrary to the USDA, Farm Bureau, and U.S. agribusiness, it is not American capitalist agriculture that points a way forward for working people, or shows how science and technology can be put to use to feed humanity and advance broader social needs. To the contrary, the only such example in today's world are the workers and farm-

---

18. The trend has continued, as after-tax profits for ADM and ConAgra rose 18 percent and 23 percent respectively between 2000 and 2002, while net farm income in the United States was down 26 percent over that same period and total farm debt rose 9 percent.

ers advancing the socialist revolution in Cuba. More than four decades ago, the revolutionary government in Cuba expropriated the capitalist landowners and nationalized the land, thereby guaranteeing farmers the right to till it for as long as they wanted. No farmer in Cuba can lose his or her land through foreclosure or a forced sale to pay off debts. The socialist government continues to provide cheap credit to farmers, as well as invaluable technical assistance in making a collective go of it on the land.

One accomplishment of which Cuban farmers and workers are justly very proud is the mechanization of sugarcane harvesting. No such machine had ever before been manufactured anywhere, since throughout the capitalist world agricultural labor gangs to perform this backbreaking work were so plentiful and consequently their wages desperately low. Plantation owners and other capitalist farm owners found it more profitable to press these workers into service at harvest time, leaving them without steady jobs or income during the "dead season," sometimes as long as nine months out of the year.

Cuba's revolutionary government, on the other hand, began organizing production in countryside and city to meet the needs of working people, not to maximize the profits of landlords and capitalists. Mechanization of the harvest was among its central goals from the outset, said Cuban president Fidel Castro in his report to the First Congress of the Communist Party of Cuba in December 1975. "In this country, we could no longer tolerate an army of unemployed, that had risen from 600,000 in 1953 to 700,000 in 1958, part of which worked on the harvest four months in the year," Castro said. He continued:

This was a typically capitalist method of sugar production, and it could only exist under the [U.S.-

"The most important lesson to be learned from Cuba is not agricultural techniques. It is what workers and farmers can accomplish when we organize a successful fight for state power and use our conquests to join in the international struggle for socialism."

TOP: Revolutionary Cuba developed the world's first mechanized sugarcane harvester, freeing hundreds of thousands of peasants from that backbreaking labor. Photo shows Ernesto Che Guevara, then minister of industry, testing the first prototype harvester, Cuba, 1963.

Alberto Korda

BOTTOM: In face of imperialist pressures, working people have initiated urban vegetable gardens across Cuba to provide fresh produce to schools, hospitals, workplace cafeterias, and population as a whole. Shown here, one such *organopónico* in Havana, 2003.

Granma

backed Batista] regime's subhuman conditions. But the country had no machine-building industry, and under the existing conditions our mechanized harvesting techniques were absolutely embryonic. Such machines simply had neither been designed nor built by modern industry. Che [Guevara] was one of the leading advocates of this endeavor.

The revolutionary government gave top priority to designing several successively more effective sugarcane harvesting combines and began manufacturing them, giving a boost to the country's industrialization. Cuba also licensed a German company to manufacture these combines; as of 1989 it had sold hundreds of them to customers in forty-four countries. By the early 1980s more than half the sugarcane harvest in Cuba had been mechanized, as had almost all the lifting of the cut cane. Machinery is also used by sugar workers to clear the canefields of scrap, making it possible for them to perform other tasks with less backbreaking labor.

Since the economic crisis that hit them so hard during the opening years of the 1990s, Cuban toilers have had to carry out agricultural production in face of reduced resources. But they have put their ingenuity to work to use whatever they have at hand—be it a tractor or a team of oxen, be it precious imported fertilizer or a sugarcane residue—to organize labor in town and country to feed and clothe the population and maintain the revolution's proletarian internationalist political course.

The job is to make a revolution
That accomplishment underlines the fact that the most important lesson to be learned in Cuba by farmers or other working people and youth from abroad is not ag-

ricultural techniques—organic or otherwise. It is what workers and farmers can accomplish anywhere in the world when we organize a successful revolutionary fight for state power and use our conquests to join in the international struggle for socialism.

Communist leader Ernesto Che Guevara once told a gathering of medical students in Cuba that "to be a revolutionary doctor . . . there must first be a revolution." That, Guevara said, is the "fundamental thing" he as a young doctor had come to understand half a decade earlier in deciding to join in the revolutionary war to free Cuba from the boot of imperialist oppression and capitalist exploitation.[19] To be a revolutionary farmer or a revolutionary worker, the same holds true. The "fundamental thing" in either case is to join in the proletarian movement to make a revolution and become a disciplined militant in its ranks.

F REDERICK ENGELS MADE A SIMILAR POINT nearly a century earlier in his article on "The Part Played by Labor in the Transition from Ape to Man." At every step along the advance of society, he wrote, human beings "are reminded that we by no means rule over nature like a conqueror over a foreign people, like someone standing outside nature—but that we, with flesh, blood, and brain, belong to nature, and exist in its midst, and that all our mastery of it consists in the fact that we have the advantage over all other creatures of being able to know and correctly apply its laws." Doing so, however, "requires something more than mere knowledge," Engels said. "It

---

19. Ernesto Che Guevara, *Che Guevara Talks to Young People* (New York: Pathfinder, 2000), p. 52 [2011 printing].

requires a complete revolution in our hitherto existing mode of production, and with it of our whole contemporary social order."[20]

It is along that road that working people will reach the end toward which they are inevitably marching: the dictatorship of the proletariat. That, in turn, will open the road to advance toward the conscious goal described in the Communist Manifesto as a "combination of agriculture with manufacturing industries" through the "gradual abolition of all the distinction between town and country." It is then, to paraphrase the Manifesto, that humanity will truly discover what immense "productive forces slumbered in the lap of social labor."[21]

---

20. Engels, *The Origin of the Family, Private Property, and the State*, pp. 272 and 274.

21. Marx and Engels, *The Communist Manifesto* (New York: Pathfinder, 1987, 2008), pp. 57 and 37 [2010 printing].

The Communist Manifesto

Karl Marx, Frederick Engels

Why communism is not a set of preconceived principles but the line of march of the working class toward power, "springing from an existing class struggle, a historical movement going on under our very eyes." The founding document of the modern revolutionary workers movement. $5. Also in Spanish, French, and Arabic.

Labor's Role in the Transition from Ape to Man

Frederick Engels

Human beings' mastery of nature, Engels writes in this 1876 article, "consists in the fact that we have the advantage over all other creatures of being able to know and correctly apply its laws." Doing so, however, "requires a complete revolution in our hitherto existing mode of production, and our whole contemporary social order." Published as an appendix to Engels's classic book, *The Origin of the Family, Private Property, and the State.* $18

Critique of the Gotha Program
by *Karl Marx*

"Labor is not the source of all wealth. Nature is just as much the source of use values as labor, which itself is only the manifestation of a force of nature, human labor power." In Marx-Engels *Collected Works,* vol. 24, $35

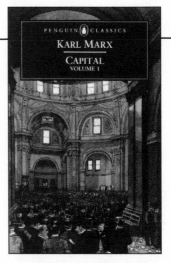

Capital
Karl Marx

Labor, Marx writes, is "a process between man and nature, a process by which…he acts upon external nature and changes it, and in this way he simultaneously changes his own nature." Marx explains the workings of the capitalist system and how it produces the insoluble contradictions that breed class struggle. He demonstrates the inevitability of the fight for the revolutionary transformation of society into one ruled for the first time by the producing majority: the working class. Vol. 1, $18; vol. 2, $18; vol. 3, $18

Problems of Everyday Life
Leon Trotsky

Articles from the early Soviet press on social and cultural issues in the struggle to forge new social relations. The advance of culture, Trotsky notes, requires an increasing level of scientific, technological, and industrial development to "free humanity from a dependence upon nature that is degrading"—a goal that can only be completed when social relationships are "free from mystery and do not oppress people." $28

Marxism and the Working Farmer
Frederick Engels, V.I. Lenin, Fidel Castro, Doug Jenness

Includes "The Peasant Question in France and Germany" by Frederick Engels, "Theses on the Agrarian Question" by V.I. Lenin, "Cuba's Agrarian Reform" by Fidel Castro, and "American Agriculture and the Working Farmer" by Doug Jenness. $7

The Workers and Farmers Government

JOSEPH HANSEN

How experiences in post–World War II revolutions in Yugoslavia, China, Algeria, and Cuba enriched communists' theoretical and practical understanding of revolutionary governments of the workers and farmers. "What is involved is governmental power," writes Hansen, "the possibility of smashing the old structure and overturning capitalism." $10

For a Workers and Farmers Government in the United States

JACK BARNES

Why a workers and farmers government is "the most powerful instrument the working class can wield" as it moves toward expropriating the capitalists and landlords. How this opens the road for working people to join in the worldwide struggle for socialism. $10

Dynamics of the Cuban Revolution

A Marxist Appreciation

JOSEPH HANSEN

How did the Cuban Revolution unfold? Why does it represent an "unbearable challenge" to US imperialism? What political obstacles has it overcome? Written as the revolution advanced from its earliest days. $25

The Rise and Fall of the Nicaraguan Revolution

JACK BARNES, LARRY SEIGLE, STEVE CLARK

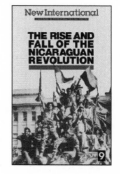

Based on ten years of socialist journalism from inside Nicaragua, this issue of *New International* magazine recounts the achievements and worldwide impact of the 1979 Nicaraguan revolution. It traces the political retreat of the Sandinista National Liberation Front leadership that led to the downfall of the workers and farmers government in the closing years of the 1980s. Documents of the Socialist Workers Party. $16

www.pathfinderpress.com

The working-class fight for power

CAPITALISM, LABOR, AND THE TRANSFORMATION OF NATURE

Following the August 2001 publication in the *Militant* of the four-part series by Steve Clark printed on the preceding pages, Richard Levins, a professor of population sciences and researcher at the Harvard School of Public Health, sent an article to the paper addressing a number of issues raised in the series. Levins is active in the July 26 Coalition, a Boston-area Cuba solidarity organization, and works with the Institute of Ecology and Systematics of the Cuban Ministry of Science, Technology and the Environment.

Levins's article, published here for the first time, is followed by a rejoinder from Clark and two final comments. Footnotes are the responsibility of *New International*.

A 'LEFT' CRITIC OF ORGANIC FARMING

by Richard Levins

THE SERIES OF FOUR ARTICLES by Steve Clark discusses a number of questions about capitalism, imperialism, and agriculture on which we can all agree easily. But the focus of his polemic is against organic agriculture and his rejection of the suggestion that its adoption in Cuba may be something more than an emergency measure. It was in part motivated by a letter from Karl Butts, who was worried that the ending of a previous article in the *Militant* seems to be giving "a certain political weight to the concept of organic production being preferable to that where chemicals are used," and that readers "may also come away thinking Cuba generally chooses not to use chemicals in agricultural production."

I think Clark got it all wrong practically, in terms of the actual technical advantages of ecological agriculture, and theoretically.

The adoption of ecological (and more narrowly organic) methods of food production in Cuba started before the Special Period, or else its rapid spread would not have been possible. It started as experimental projects in a number of institutions because the researchers realized

that "modern" high-tech agriculture
- undermined its own productive base through soil erosion, compaction, and salinization, reducing soil organic matter and nitrogen-fixing capacity, increasing the need for irrigation;
- increased vulnerability to pests and disease, requiring ever-bigger and more frequent doses of pesticides;
- increased vulnerability to the uncertainties of the weather and economy;
- poisoned farmers and farmworkers (for instance brain cancer is more prevalent in the areas that use the herbicide atrazine);
- contaminated the ground waters and soil; and
- made the farm dependent on external inputs.

Projects in ecological pest management, polyculture, biofertilization, recycling of farm wastes, integration of crops and livestock, and the redesign of farm tools and machines were undertaken at many different research centers. This is not "a reject[ion of] progress in agricultural chemistry and technology in favor of so-called natural or traditional methods of farming." It is a modern, scientific, dialectical activity of knowledge-creation, using and testing critically the knowledge of the peasants along with modern experimental, observational, and mathematical approaches. When the Special Period came, we had at least a starting point for a new technology. And there is no doubt that it saved the revolution. But will this continue? Is it a second-best improvisation imposed by the economic crisis, as Clark believes, or a better production system? Nilda Pérez and Luis Vázquez, in a forthcoming book on Cuban agriculture deal with this:

> Everyone asks what will become of ecological
> pest management in Cuba as we emerge from

the economic crisis of the early 1990s. As more foreign exchange becomes available for the purchase of pesticides on the international market it seems logical to some that Cuba will return to an intensive dependence on chemical inputs. Moreover, some think the current program of accelerated reduction of pesticides is simply a short-term, stop-gap answer to maintain production until pesticide imports are affordable once again. But others—and they are more than a few—have a very different analysis, looking seriously at economic, social, health, and environmental factors, and conclude that the agroecological IPM [integrated pest management—RL] model developed to date is simply a better model. . . . In light of recent history, it is hard to believe that Cuba would return to the calendar sprayings of the 1960s and early 1970s or even to (chemical) dependence of the 1980s.[1]

In 1997, the Cuban Ministry of Science, Technology, and the Environment organized a "Rio+5" national consultation workshop to evaluate Cuban compliance with the Rio accords (Agenda 21) on the environment.[2] For each aspect of the national environment plan such as

1. The book has subsequently been published. Fernando Funes, Luis García, Martin Bourque, Nilda Pérez and Peter Rosset, eds., *Sustainable Agriculture and Resistance: Transforming Food Production in Cuba* (Oakland, Calif.: Food First Books, 2002).—Ed.

2. The 1992 United Nations Conference on Environment and Development, or Earth Summit, held in Rio de Janeiro, Brazil, adopted an action plan called Agenda 21. In 1997 governments that participated in the Earth Summit organized conferences to assess implementation of those goals over the previous five years; these were often referred to as "Rio+5" gatherings.—Ed.

resisting desertification, sustainable development of the mountainous regions, and sustainable agriculture, achievements were listed, difficulties identified, and proposals made. One obstacle to the development of sustainable agriculture was "the existence of the opinion, at various levels, that the practice of a sustainable agriculture is only a consequence of the Special Period and is destined to disappear when the present limitations make it possible and there will be a return to the high inputs of fertilizers, pesticides, mechanization, etc." Thus, there were people who shared Clark's views, but this was regarded as retrograde by at least the middle 1990s.

What makes agroecology a better model? Contrary to the claims of the high-tech boosters, it is economical. For instance, a comparison of costs of biological and chemical control of pests in Cuba showed that in horticultural crops biological control cost about one-third the cost of chemical control, in grasses one-eighth, in plantain one-tenth, in rice one-third.

The biological control included the raising and release of beneficial insects, fungi, and bacteria; application of extracts of botanicals; enhancement of local natural enemies of pests; and other methods. One reason for the economical performance is that whereas spraying has to be repeated regularly, once ants are introduced into a banana plantation they spread throughout it in about six weeks and then protect the crop at least as well as the repeated spraying does. There is still room for further cost reduction as we move from input substitution to ecosystem design.

Intercropping of different kinds of plants in the same field is partly for pest control but also has other advantages, and in the right combinations is more productive than monoculture. We represent this increased productivity by the LER (land equivalency ratio), the amount of land in monoculture needed to get the same yield as one hectare of intercropping. For instance, one hectare of intercropped cassava, tomato, and maize yields as much as almost two hectares of these crops planted separately. Finally, I want to cite the integration of animals with crops. For instance seven to thirteen sheep grazing in a hectare of citrus grove produce some 343–596 kg live weight without harming citrus production, while horses can play a major role in weed suppression in citrus. Geese did not work well—they nibbled the leaves of young trees.

Studies in the United States and other countries also show that organic methods are usually at least as good as the high-tech, especially when the weather conditions are unfavorable.

CONTRARY TO THE CAPITALIST notion of efficiency through specialized monocultures, the future of Cuban agriculture will be a mosaic of land uses in which each area, besides providing some harvestable products, also contributes to the production of other areas. Forests yield wood, honey, and nuts; modulate the flow of water so as to reduce dependence on pumping irrigation water; are a refuge for beneficial insects, birds, and bats; and create special microclimates around their edges to a distance of about ten times the height of the trees. Pastures produce livestock but also retard erosion compared to row crops, produce manure and house swarms of pollinators and predators, and so on. The sizes of these patches depends on the physical conditions, the landscape, the mobility of the relevant insects, and similar factors. So there is no absolute rule that large scale is economical and modern while small is backward, nor is there an absolute rule that "small is beautiful." The ecology dictates the sizes of units of production within the larger units of planning.

Cubans and researchers in other countries have shown that ecological and organic production methods can be more productive, more economical, and certainly more protective of the environment and the workers and consumers than high-tech methods considered as the most "modern" in the capitalist world. Organic methods are being extended gradually as the appropriate techniques are developed. There are now projects for the development of organic production of sugar, coffee, citrus, and other export crops. The new methods have to be introduced gradually, with careful preparation of technicians and farmers so that it will be done correctly. Not any old combination of crops gives good yield; desisting from spraying chemicals is not organic pest control; and careless introduction of what seem like OK ideas could discredit the whole program. Therefore, at present most agriculture includes a mixture of organic and semi-organic methods with progressive reduction of chemical use, while urban agriculture is almost totally organic. Roughly half of Cuba's vegetable production is organic, as is all the urban production. Butts is right that chemicals are used in the production of sugar, rice, coffee, and indeed of other crops. But for all of them, there are programs for the reduction of chemical inputs. Transplanting of rice and mulching of sugarcane are weed-control methods that reduce herbicides. Wasps are raised in on-farm insectaries for use against the sugarcane borer. The whole strategy is one of progressive reduction of chemical inputs as the alternatives are developed.

Perhaps it is unfair to use data to which Clark had no access. And yet the core of the Marxist methodology is to start with the concrete and build theoretical argument from real experience. Clark got it all wrong empirically and also methodologically and theoretically. Perhaps the core error is his view of scientific and technical progress.

SCIENCE AND TECHNOLOGY have a dual nature: they are certainly part of the general development of the knowledge and capability of the human species. But they are also the specific products of particular societies and meet the goals of the owners of those societies. This gives rise to a pattern of knowledge and ignorance chosen by the owners of the knowledge industry who recruit the scientists, set the research agendas, and determine the uses of science. It is necessary to acknowledge both aspects of this contradiction and therefore both to appreciate modern science and to criticize it. Marx and Engels were enthusiastic advocates of Darwin, yet also criticized his Whig (that is, liberal) gradualism. The Science for the People movement in the 1960s–1970s in this country and similar groups internationally have struggled with this reality. Their perspective advanced from a criticism of the misuses of science for war, to a criticism of the exclusion of working-class people, Afro-Americans, and women of all races from scientific leadership, to finally an examination of the very content of the science as it evolves according to the needs of industry and the prevailing philosophies. In the end, the struggle between high-tech chemicalized agriculture and ecological agriculture is also between mechanistic/reductionist and dialectical views of nature and of science.

But too often socialists fall into a passive progressivism that sees only one side of the contradiction, imagines only one pathway of progress along which things are either more advanced or more backward. Then they imagine that capitalist technique can be adopted lock, stock, and barrel to socialist ends. This admiration of bourgeois technology without also an active critique of that technology was one of the elements in the disastrous history of Soviet industry. (These technical choices in turn could of course be linked to evolving class structures in that country. The uncritical admiration for capitalist pathways of development reached their extreme in Brezhnev's reliance on the "scientific-technical revolution" to save the Soviet Union.) With this approach it is possible to sneer, with Clark, at the use of animal traction as having been a novelty in Neolithic times and to misrepresent the critique of capitalist technology as anti-science. The reality is that agricultural science and technology developed to invent those production methods which can be commodities for sale to farmers, and within the framework of capitalist reductionist philosophy.

The major steps in the advance of agricultural methods were: the adoption of the industrial steam engine as a stationary energy source for threshing in the nineteenth century; from the automobile industry the differential gear that gave us the tractor for mechanization; from surplus gunpowder productive capacity after the First World War to nitrogen fixation and chemical fertilizer; from chemical warfare in the First World War to pesticides; and finally with modern plant breeding a branch of research designed specifically for agriculture. Plant breeders aimed at the creation of hybrid seed not because that is the best way to improve yield but because hybrid seed do not breed true, and farmers would have to buy a new supply of hybrid seed every year. The particular pattern of research reflects the fact that not all knowledge is equally commodifiable. A toxic chemical can be bottled and sold to farmers whereas knowledge of predatory ants can at most be sold as a Hints for Farm and Garden column.

Even within the framework of capitalist development, new methods do not simply replace old ones. Rather the older forms that were universal now become specialized and continue to evolve. There is still a role for propeller aircraft, sailboats, hand tools. Modern medicine does not replace herbal medicine but can incorporate it. And Cuban farmers have found that animal traction has its place. Oxen have a different impact on the soil from tractors and are able to work after heavy rains where tractors would only destroy the soil. The idea is not to replace mechanization but to combine it with animal use as appropriate. In my youth I farmed in the central cordillera of Puerto Rico on land too steep for tractors or even oxen. So I have no sentimental nostalgia for the backbreaking work of preparing a heavy clay soil with a hoe nor yearn for Neolithic simplicity. And I can tell the difference between reverting to less effective technologies and inventing new ones that incorporate past knowledge.

Every society develops its own way of relating to the rest of nature and of conceiving of that relation. Cuban socialism is creating its own ecology—a landscape that brings agriculture into the cities and industry to the countryside; designs a food production system that is robust in the face of uncertainty; is protective of people's health; preserves biodiversity, water resources, and soil; recycles within the farm and regionally; and is minimally dependent on external inputs. It is doing this in many ways— through programs against desertification and salinization, through reforestation, integration of cropping and livestock, ecological agriculture, and is supported by a creative network of professional and nonprofessional innovators. There is a growing realization in Cuba that the rising standard of living to which we all aspire will not be achieved by unlimited increases in the consumption of energy and matter but in a rising quality of life in which a better relation with the rest of nature is an important element. Ecological agriculture is one aspect of an emerging socialist pattern of relating to the rest of nature, a new mode of eco-social production.

The social role of organic agriculture in the United States is quite different from that in Cuba. The present organic movement represents a coming together of organic growers, looking for reduced dependence on the corporations, some of whom are of urban origin and chose farming for lifestyle reasons, consumer co-ops and other groups concerned with quality food, health advocates who saw pesticides as carcinogens and destroyers of biodiversity, and agricultural scientists who would have liked to farm but can't afford to buy land, who dedicate themselves instead to serving the organic community.

In the Northeast, NOFA (Northeast Organic Farming Association) links small producers, artisans, consumer groups, and innovators in a generally progressive movement in conflict with monopolized agriculture. They have been inventing ways of reducing costs so that the working people of our cities can also get the better-quality food they deserve. But as organic farming becomes more popular, big investors become interested, and there has been a struggle within organic farming between capitalist commercial growers and the initiators of the movement. Recently this conflict has focused on the rules of certification of organic food. The USDA has taken control of certification away from the organic farming organizations and has pushed for lower standards more congenial to the big producers.

Clark rejects organic farming as an idealist solution. But a solution to what? He sets up a straw petty bourgeois when he suggests that organic farming under capitalism is offered as an alternative to revolutionary struggle. It is "merely" a struggle for safer food production and better-quality food.

Finally, there is the question of the genetically modified organisms (GMOs). Clark endorses them as a way to produce abundance in a hungry world. He thinks he found a great inconsistency in the critics of genetically engineered crops when he points out that critics of GMOs in agriculture did not criticize the use of genetically modified bacteria to produce insulin. The obvious difference between these two cases is that if something goes wrong in the industrial production of insulin it is possible to shut down the fermenters and clean them out, but if things go wrong in nature they cannot be recalled so easily. The issue is not one of principle, "for" or "against" GMOs. Rather it is one of applying four tests before accepting a technology:

1. *Is it necessary?* In this case, is world hunger caused by the lack of food or productive capacity? According to the UN's World Food Programme, there is enough food in the world today for twelve billion people. Despite local and regional crop failures that do cause hunger, the basic cause is that food is a commodity and that the need for food is not supported by "effective demand," that farmers are displaced by agribusiness aiming at high-value export crops, that people are displaced from the land by wars and price squeezes, and that production is aimed at

profit, not feeding people.

2. *Would the new technology do what it promises?* Here the results are ambiguous. Initial successes in laboratory trials are sometimes offset in the field when other factors enter.

3. *What else does it do?* We know some of the obvious effects: tightening the control of the chemical monopolies over food production and over farmers, promoting monocultures that increase the dangers of pests. By building into the crops genes for pest resistance the new varieties present the pests with pesticides even when they are not a problem, encouraging a more rapid evolution of pesticide resistance. The transfer of herbicide resistance from crops to weeds can produce herbicide-resistant weeds. And there are other, less probable but more disastrous possibilities coming from the fact that introduced genes are mobile genes, and that when genes change their location in the genome their effects can be quite different from what they did at home. The point here is not that any particular introduction will cause a disaster but that the urge to patent and market products in a hurry makes industry and their allies in government belittle potential harm, not look for unexpected consequences, and cover up hints of harm.

4. *Are there better alternatives?* Here the answer is a definite yes. Even with so much less research going into organic methods than chemical methods the results are comparable. Ecologically sound agrotechnology is more stable, protects the environment from pollution of ground waters and the air, protects farmworkers and consumers, reduces farmer dependence on the chemical companies and therefore slows down the impoverishment of the countryside.

On the whole, Clark replaces a socialist view of the complexities of scientific and technological development with a one-sided liberal progressivist approach that accepts capitalism's claim that "There IS No Alternative." But a revolutionary movement has to challenge the destructive, alienating nature of all aspects of capitalist society in order to build the kind of movement that can liberate the working class and the whole of society.

PROGRESS FOR WHOM?

by Steve Clark

I N HIS REPLY Richard Levins begins by asserting that the *Militant* articles discuss "a number of questions about capitalism, imperialism, and agriculture on which we can all easily agree." As indicated by its title, however, the *Militant* series deals not with "capitalism, imperialism, and agriculture" in the abstract, but with *labor* and agriculture, *labor* and imperialism, *labor* and capitalism, whether in the fields, factories, mines, mills, or elsewhere. And it is precisely these social relations—involving the working class and the political and social foundations of the worker-farmer alliance—that are absent from Levins's reply. It is there we find the heart of our disagreement.

To the degree workers and farmers make an appearance in Levins's article, they are victims of poisonous pesticides, recipients of services by researchers and scientists, or beneficiaries of movements that will provide them wholesome food and pave the way for their liberation. Working people as the producers of all wealth through the transformation of nature, the creators of the material basis of culture and civilization, and the agents

of their and humanity's liberation through revolutionary struggle to establish the proletarian dictatorship are
not present.

Levins argues that the *Militant* series puts forward an
erroneous view "of scientific and technical progress." The
articles are marked, he says, by "a one-sided liberal progressivist approach that accepts capitalism's claim that
'There IS No Alternative.'"

COMMUNISTS PLEAD GUILTY to holding the view that
so long as the capitalist rulers hold state power, there
will be no alternative mode of production: none that
serves the interests of urban and rural working people.
None that will prevent the inevitable outcome of capitalist domination—concentration of productive property
in fewer and fewer hands, penury for the many, fascism,
war, even nuclear conflagration. And communists plead
guilty to being students of Lenin's strategic observation
and guide that no lasting reform of the consequences of
capitalist social relations is possible in our epoch save as
a by-product of revolutionary class struggle.

That's why the *Militant* articles reaffirmed the relationship between labor and nature first highlighted by Marx
and Engels in the Communist Manifesto and later elaborated in *Capital* and elsewhere.[1] "Labor is not the source
of all wealth," wrote Marx in the "Critique of the Gotha
Program" in 1875. "Nature is just as much the source of
use values (and it is surely of such that material wealth
consists!) as labor, which itself is only the manifestation
of a force of nature, human labor power.... [I]nsofar as

---

1. Marx and Engels, *The Communist Manifesto*, pp. 57 and 37;
Capital, vol. 1, p. 283.

man from the beginning behaves toward nature, the primary source of all instruments and subjects of labor, as an owner, treats her as belonging to him, his labor becomes the source of use values, therefore also of wealth."[2]

All human labor, moreover, is organized within specific social relations of production, which are themselves reproduced by production under those class relations.

Levins's descriptions of various methods of agricultural production are abstracted from the social relations on which they depend. He writes, for example, that "one hectare of intercropped cassava, tomato, and maize yields as much as almost two hectares of these crops planted separately." But in the production of food, which is a social process, a hectare of cassava, tomatoes, and maize, in and of itself, yields nothing. It is farmers and farmworkers who sow and harvest cassava, tomatoes, and maize, reproducing as they do so the social relations of production under which they live and work. (Each of these particular farm products in its modern edible form, in fact, is the outcome of crossbreeding and processing by human labor over centuries and successive modes of production.) Levins says that "seven to thirteen sheep grazing in a hectare of citrus grove produce some 343–596 kg live weight without harming citrus production." But the sheep produce nothing. Farmers and farmworkers raise sheep, and the class relations and conditions under which they do so determine to a great degree the live weight attained and the impact on the cultivation of other farm products.

Levins writes that "forests yield wood, honey, and nuts" and "modulate the flow of water so as to reduce dependence on pumping irrigation water." Likewise "pastures

2. "Critique of the Gotha Programme," in Marx, Engels, *Collected Works*, vol. 24, p. 81.

produce livestock but also retard erosion." But it is social labor that transforms forests into wood; honey and nuts into food; and livestock into beasts of burden, a source of nourishment, or hides for clothing and other uses. The way such labor is organized, the class relations governing the productive activity of working people, either accelerate or retard erosion, either increase or reduce irrigation-related damage to the soil and waters.

Lessons from Cuban Revolution

Levins provides an informative account of agricultural accomplishments in Cuba before and during the Special Period (accomplishments, in fact, of farmers, agricultural workers, technicians, and organizers). He identifies the source of these achievements, however, as the use of particular farming methods, not the fact that Cuban working people overturned capitalist social relations at the opening of the 1960s and continue to this day along the road they set out on—in the words of Ernesto Che Guevara, "simultaneous with the new material foundation, to build the new man."[3] The same agricultural technologies applied either by labor on capitalist farms, or by working farmers subordinate to the capitalist rents and mortgages system, do not lead to the same social results. "The most important lesson to be learned in Cuba by farmers or other working people and youth from abroad," the *Militant* articles concluded, "is not agricultural techniques—organic or otherwise. It is what workers and farmers can accomplish anywhere in the world when we organize a successful revolutionary fight for state power and use our conquests

---

3. Ernesto Che Guevara, "Socialism and Man in Cuba," in *Che Guevara Speaks* (New York: Pathfinder, 1967, 2000), p. 158 [2011 printing].

to join in the international struggle for socialism."

Levins fetishizes particular farming methods. "When the Special Period came, we had at least a starting point for a new technology," he writes. "And there is no doubt that *it* saved the revolution" [emphasis added].

But it was not "a new technology" that "saved" the Cuban Revolution in face of the Stalinist death rattle in the Soviet Union and Eastern Europe, and sudden collapse of Cuba's quarter-century-long trade patterns in the early 1990s. The staying power of the Cuban Revolution is rooted in the political consciousness and mobilization of workers and farmers in their millions, manifested in many ways—from their readiness to defend the revolution arms in hand, to their proletarian internationalism, to their ingenuity and creativity on many fronts of life and labor, agricultural production among them.

"Cubans and researchers in other countries," Levins writes, "have shown that ecological and organic production methods can be more productive, more economical, and certainly more protective of the environment and the workers and consumers than high-tech methods considered the most 'modern' in the capitalist world."

But "methods" are not productive, economical, or protective. It is social labor that is productive, or not. It is human beings who develop, modify, and *use* various methods to transform nature and create social wealth. It is human beings who either do or don't keep track of costs adequately. It is human beings who can organize production in ways that protect workers and the natural environment. These are class questions—their morals and ours—the social solidarity defended by toilers and our allies versus the private appropriation of social wealth, the dog-eat-dog motor force of all class society.

"Cuban socialism" is not "creating its own ecology," as

Levins argues, once again substituting an abstraction for the concrete class relations involved. (Engels, with a twinkle in his eye, might have recommended a close rereading of "The Fetishism of Commodities and Its Secret" in volume one of Marx's *Capital*.) It is *Cuban working people* who are creating something new as they defend, advance, and transform their social relations of production, transforming themselves in the process. As they do so, they are deciding what kind of fertilizers, pest controls, and other tools to use under the objective conditions they face. There is nothing abstract about it.

Levins concludes that "there is no absolute rule that large scale is economical and modern while small is backward, nor is there an absolute rule that 'small is beautiful.'" Agreed. And that's important, since for much of the twentieth century the dominant voices falsely claiming to speak on behalf of world communism—the Stalinist misleaderships in Moscow and Beijing—rationalized their brutal, bureaucratic policies toward rural toilers in the name of "economic necessity." Even in Cuba, the "large-scale-is-economical-and-modern" orthodoxy was a contributing factor (though far from the cause) of the agricultural crises workers and farmers began addressing in 1986 with the opening of what Cubans call the rectification process.

Levins himself, in his 1985 book co-authored by Richard Lewontin, *The Dialectical Biologist*, argued that "Chinese agriculture rapidly passed from cooperative to collective chiefly by persuasion and local voluntarism"—a Maoist myth the *Militant* refuted in the late 1950s as the forced march into so-called people's communes got under way, and that few today would defend. That same book apologized for Stalin's forced collectivization of the peasantry in the Soviet Union in the late 1920s and early 1930s, saying it was "required by a rational socialist economy" and "the pressing demand to feed the urban working population." Levins placed blame for the resulting devastation of Soviet agriculture on the peasants' acts of self-defense, calling their destruction of crops and livestock "wrecking" and "sabotage to protect their private property." "This force was met with greater and more terrible force by the state, which eventually won the day [!] for collectivization," Levins wrote, "but at a great cost in lives, material wealth, and political development."[4]

THE STALINIST REGIME's forced collectivization was the opposite of the course advocated by Lenin of encouraging the voluntary organization of farm cooperatives in the Soviet Union, whose existence was grounded in a class alliance of the workers and peasants. "Link up with the peasant masses, with the rank-and-file working peasants, and begin to move forward immeasurably, infinitely more slowly than we expected, but in such a way that the entire mass will actually move forward with us," Lenin told delegates to a party congress in March 1922. "We must prove . . . that in this period, when the small peasant is in a state of appalling ruin, impoverishment, and starvation, the Communists are really helping him. Either we prove that, or he will send us to the devil. That is absolutely inevitable."[5] And inevitable it became a few years later

---

4. "The Problem of Lysenkoism" in Richard Levins and Richard Lewontin, *The Dialectical Biologist* (Cambridge, Mass.: Harvard University Press, 1985), p. 182.

5. "Political Report to Eleventh Party Congress" in V.I. Lenin, *Lenin's Final Fight: Speeches and Writings, 1922–23* (New York: Pathfinder, 1995, 2010), pp. 55 and 56 [2010 printing]. In the same book, see "On Cooperation," pp. 254–62.

under the policies of the privileged caste—first favoring rich peasants over the masses of rural toilers; then, when the slogan "Peasants, enrich yourselves!" bore its predetermined poisonous fruit in the late 1920s, forcibly confiscating the livestock, implements, and land used by the peasantry as a whole, down to the smallest garden plots.

Cuba's land reform, too, followed a class course, solidifying the worker-farmer alliance on which the revolution rests—a course that represents the negation of Stalinist policy. Fidel Castro explained that policy in 1988 in his speech to the July 26 celebration in Santiago de Cuba:

> The manner in which an agrarian reform was carried out in our country differed from the manner in which all the other socialist countries carried it out. . . . We gave land to the peasant who was in possession of it, to sharecroppers, tenant farmers, and others. We said to them all, here you are, the land is yours, and subsequently we have not forced any of them to join cooperatives. The process of uniting those plots has taken us thirty years. We've gone ahead little by little on the basis of the strict principle of it being voluntary. There is not a single peasant in Cuba who can say that he was forced to join a cooperative, there is not a single one! And yet, more than two-thirds of their lands now belong to cooperatives.[6]

While Levins seems to have modified his views since 1985, his recognition that "there is no absolute rule that large scale is economical and modern" is joined to a

---

6. Fidel Castro, *'Cuba Will Never Adopt Capitalist Methods'* (New York: Pathfinder, 1988), p. 17 [2008 printing].

sentence that doesn't follow: "The ecology dictates the sizes of units of production within the larger units of planning." But the size and character of units of agricultural production in Cuba, to take that example, are the concrete outcome of several decades of experience with different forms of organization, social conflicts, debates, and political initiatives by Cuban workers, farmers, and their communist leadership. These include:

• the first and second agrarian reforms during the opening years of the revolution;

• measures adopted as part of a "socialist division of labor" imposed by the privileged caste dominating the USSR and Council for Mutual Economic Assistance (CMEA), which Cuba joined in 1972;

• the rectification process of the latter 1980s, a proletarian reorientation aimed at mobilizing the toilers to reverse declining productivity, increasing food dependency, demoralization, and other political consequences of bureaucratic policies of planning and management that had been adopted in the mid-1970s, modeled on those in the USSR; and

• revolutionary measures adopted under pressures of the Special Period, including the promotion of small-scale urban agriculture (the *organopónicos*).

The political consciousness of Cuban toilers; retreats fostering growth of privileged administrative personnel; struggles against policies favoring better-off bureaucratic layers; availability or scarcity of energy and industrial goods, determined by vicissitudes of the class struggle far beyond Cuba's borders; and the international balance of class forces, including decades of U.S. economic warfare—all these have weighed in the scales. Neither "the ecology," whatever Levins means by that, nor any other factor external to social relations has "dictated" the forms of organization of agricultural labor adopted by the Cuban government and working people today. Nor is any of these forms set in stone. They will be changed and developed in step with the social and political progress of Cuban workers and farmers as a whole.

Bourgeois technology, or bourgeois values?

Levins is concerned that some socialists (the *Militant* included?) "fall into a passive progressivism" and "imagine that capitalist technique can be adopted lock, stock, and barrel to socialist ends. This admiration of bourgeois technology without also an active critique of that technology was one of the elements in the disastrous history of Soviet industry," he writes, reaching its "extreme in Brezhnev's reliance on the 'scientific-technical revolution' to save the Soviet Union."

The lack of an "active critique" of "bourgeois technology" has little to do with what Levins euphemistically describes as "the disastrous history of Soviet industry" (there is no history of Soviet industry divorced from the history of the consequences of the Bolshevik Revolution betrayed). The roots of that disaster go back not to Soviet premier Leonid Brezhnev but to the toilers' exhaustion in face of a bloody civil war, imperialist invasions, and defeats of the post-World War I revolutionary upsurge across Europe; the emergence of privileged layers in the state and party apparatus; and the cutting short of Lenin's struggle against the political course of those layers by a debilitating stroke in early 1923. By the late 1920s a bureaucratic caste whose leading figure was Joseph Stalin had consolidated a political counterrevolution. Reversing the course of the Bolshevik Party and Communist International under Lenin's leadership, the caste subordinated domestic and foreign policy to advancing its interests,

which were alien to those of workers and peasants. Its policies were marked not primarily by "uncritical admiration
of bourgeois technology," but by the accelerated aping
of *bourgeois values* and related thuggish and bureaucratic
methods against "backward" toilers and critics in every
sphere of economic, social, and political life.

Brezhnev's demagogic appeals for a "scientific-technical
revolution" in the Soviet Union from the late 1960s through
the early 1980s were not an "extreme" point in this political degeneration but the petering out of a decades-long
trajectory. They registered the desperate, second-to-last
chapter in that course, whose earlier benchmarks in farm
policy included:

• forced collectivization, from which Soviet agriculture
never recovered (even quantitatively, grain yields and
livestock herds did not regain their 1929 levels until the
early 1950s, and peasants and farmworkers were never
able to control and administer the state farms and col-
lectives imposed on them);

• the caste's increasing rejection of the science of genetics from the mid-1930s through 1965 ("Lysenkoism"),
quackery pursued in hopes of reviving grain output in
the wake of the collectivization disaster, setting both agriculture and science still further back; and

• Soviet Communist Party leader Nikita Khrushchev's
mid-1950s surge to open "virgin lands" to cultivation on
a massive scale, a bureaucratic fiasco whose upshot was a
Dust Bowl across much of Russia within a decade.

The thread weaved throughout this record of Stalinist counterrevolution is not a philosophical debate over
"mechanistic/reductionist" versus "dialectical views of
nature and of science." The caste had no ideas—reductionist, dialectical, or those of Professor Irwin Corey. It
cranked out pragmatic rationalizations to protect its pre-

rogatives and defend its privileges. It made scapegoats out of revolutionary-minded workers and communists who fought to continue the course of Lenin and the Bolshevik Party, smearing them as "agents of Hitler," "agents of the Mikado," and later "agents of the CIA," "Trotskyites," "Zionists," "Trotskyite-Zionists," and so on. Millions were terrorized, sent to prison camps, or annihilated by Stalin's international murder machine—police-state methods used to crush all vestiges of political life and revolutionary activity among workers and peasants, which constituted the greatest threat to the caste's bureaucratic domination. The shattering of this increasingly brittle, decaying regime at the opening of the 1990s was the inevitable social consequence of a long political course.

Starting with the world

Some forty-five years ago, in face of this political counterrevolution, the Cuban Revolution and its leadership began reopening the possibility of the development and *use* of Marxism as a revolutionary guide to popular struggles by workers and farmers not just in the Americas but far beyond. That alone would give the leadership of the Cuban Revolution a special place in world history and the class struggle.

As the *Militant* articles pointed out, building proletarian parties and an international revolutionary movement—whose sole reason for being is to bring to power workers and farmers governments and advance the struggle for socialism—is impossible without fighting to close the enormous gap in economic, social, and cultural conditions among working people of different countries, and between urban and rural areas worldwide.

The majority of the planet's population still live in

the countryside, most of these rural toilers working the land. Imperialism stunts and deforms economic and social development throughout Asia, Africa, and Latin America, including the application of modern scientific farming techniques by tillers to increase their productivity. Finance capital joins with homegrown exploiters to block land reform and access to affordable credit. It makes food self-sufficiency impossible by devoting more and more land to the cultivation of export crops for the world market. Its profit drive strangles the allocation of resources to develop new strains of plants or animal life better suited to the soil, climate, and other needs of toilers the world over.

As Marx recognized nearly a century and a half ago, so long as production, credit, and marketing are determined by competition for profits, the use of mechanization, chemical fertilizers, and other advanced farming methods—*necessities* that are still out of reach for the big majority of tillers worldwide—simultaneously result in depletion of the soil, fouling of waters, and harm to the health of farmers, farmworkers, and the public. Many biological methods used by farmers in Cuba today, developed with assistance from scientists and technicians, undoubtedly have application for toilers the world over, with concrete modifications. In Cuba, however, a socialist revolution has broken the domination of capitalist social relations, enabling working people to organize collective labor to meet human needs not maximize private profits. So any broad extension to other countries of what's happening in urban and rural Cuba is first and foremost a question of revolutionary proletarian politics, not the emulation of farming methods.

"To be a revolutionary doctor," as Ernesto Che Guevara reminded medical students in Cuba in August 1960, "there must first be a revolution."[7]

The same political criteria apply to the cultivation of so-called genetically modified organisms, or GMOs. Opponents of imperialist exploitation shouldn't campaign to bar or limit development of new plant strains. We should welcome such scientific advances while exposing the inhuman irrationality of how capitalism puts them to use: the patenting of seeds by owners of companies such as Monsanto and Pioneer to intensify price-gouging of farmers; agribusiness efforts to limit GMO technology to "profitable" crops, not staples hundreds of millions depend on for their lives and livelihoods; the fraud of profit-driven testing and regulation, with all the ensuing dangers for humanity, versus proletarian standards of health and safety guided by human solidarity; protectionist trade battles among the major capitalist powers from which working people suffer devastating consequences (and that are themselves just one manifestation of increasingly strident interimperialist conflicts through which we have been able to hear the opening guns of World War III rumbling since the first Iraq War in 1991).

"The issue is not one of principle, 'for' or 'against' GMOs," Levins says, but of applying several tests "before accepting a technology." He continues: "Would the new technology do what it promises? . . . What else does it do? We know some of the obvious effects: tightening the control of the chemical monopolies over food production and over farmers, promoting monocultures that increase the dangers of pests."

Not to belabor the point, we note once again that Levins's arguments take no account of human labor and class relations. The "new technology," in and of it-

---

7. Guevara, *Che Guevara Talks to Young People*, p. 52 [2011 printing].

self, does nothing. Human beings—acting within the laws of motion of capitalism and the class struggle they engender—*use* new techniques and technologies to do things that have social consequences. The exploiters' development and promotion of genetically modified crops does tighten the domination of corporations over farmers, as does their control over the breeding and/ or production of domesticated animals, hybrid seeds, nitrogen fertilizer, threshers, tractors, and just about everything else. The competition of ever-larger capitals "promotes monocultures," "increases the dangers of pests"—and much worse, in field, mine, and factory, and on a world arena.

As THE ORIGINAL SERIES of articles in the *Militant* underscored, citing the words of Marx, "It took both time and experience before the workers learned to distinguish between machinery and its employment by capital, and therefore to transfer their attacks from the material instruments of production to the form of society which utilizes those instruments."

The Cuban government is currently conducting research and development of genetically modified potatoes, rice, corn, sugarcane, sweet potatoes, papaya, and tilapia, a freshwater fish. An article in the July 13, 2004, online edition of *Granma International*, for example, pointed out that addressing drought conditions in regions of Cuba "is not just a matter of using less water; rather, it also implies the use of genetic methods to obtain strains that are more resistant to water scarcity."

Carlos Borroto, deputy director of the Genetic Engineering and Biotechnology Center, described Cuba's research program in a roundtable discussion among scientists that took place in Havana a couple of years ago.[8] "We have worked for more than fifteen years with technologically modified microorganisms and we do not yet have a single plant in commercial use," Borroto said. "This is precisely because we are carrying out a risk assessment. I can say with absolute certainty that, as with any other modern technology with risks, these risks are completely controllable, if managed well."

The Cuban government's decision to not yet release any transgenic products is also due in part to interimperialist trade rivalries that have led governments in Europe to stoke public fears of GMOs to rationalize import bans or barriers. "We don't want to be the first to release a transgenic fish into the world!" Borroto told a March 2004 conference in London, according to a report in the April issue of *Cuba Sí*, magazine of the Cuba Solidarity Campaign in the United Kingdom. He also pointed to the example of an importer in Europe who rejected considering Cuban tobacco with a gene resistant to blue mould because "cigar lovers would not buy cigars made from a GM plant! I find this position somewhat strange," the Cuban scientist commented, "given the known dangers of smoking, that people should be concerned at the risk of GM!"

The 'organic movement'

Contrary to Levins's impression, the *Militant* articles were not a defense of any particular farming method in Cuba

8. In Fidel Castro Díaz-Balart (ed.) *Cuba, Amanecer del Tercer Milenio. Ciencia, sociedad y tecnología* [Cuba, Dawn of the Third Millennium: Science, Society, and Technology] (Havana: Editorial Científico-Técnica, 2002), p. 257. Borroto is also head of the National Agricultural Biotechnology Program in Cuba.

or anywhere else, by any workforce or under any social system. That is beyond the competence of their author. Responding to a letter to the editor, the articles pointed out that Cuban farmers continue to apply chemical as well as biological fertilizers and other farm inputs. Levins confirms this fact, saying that "most agriculture [in Cuba] includes a mixture of organic and semiorganic methods with progressive reduction of chemical use, while urban agriculture is almost totally organic."

The articles continued (and here Levins differs) that "as improved economic conditions enable them to do so, the Cuban government and people will undoubtedly choose once again to increase the use of such chemical farm inputs and technologies as are relatively safe, if doing so helps farmers and farmworkers increase productivity, reduce backbreaking labor, and feed and clothe more people at lower cost." The articles also expressed the view that Cuban farmers, as fuel becomes more affordable, will again increase the use of motorized farm machinery and reduce widespread reliance on oxen imposed by necessity in recent years—something that not only lowers productivity of farm labor but wears on human muscle and bone.

Levins says he has "no sentimental nostalgia for the backbreaking work of preparing a heavy clay soil with a hoe," does not "yearn for a Neolithic simplicity," and "can tell the difference between reverting to less effective technologies and inventing new ones that incorporate past knowledge." Good. We have no dispute there. But the same cannot be said for many in the so-called organic movement in the United States that Levins champions in his reply.

As a *political* course, "organic farming" has become predominantly a cause of professionals and the better-off middle classes who dream of a kinder, gentler capitalism. For many it is a lifestyle choice they have the discretionary income and option to pursue. As a business, it is a growing, high-priced, and increasingly monopolized specialty niche in the capitalist food industry, one that numerous struggling farmers have turned towards in hopes of holding on to their land, health, livelihood, and profit margins. Either way, its goals and composition are alien to a proletarian line of march that educates and mobilizes a revolutionary *anticapitalist* movement of the working class and its exploited and oppressed allies among farmers, fishermen, other producers, and the middle classes.

LEVINS READS THE *Militant* series as setting up a straw man—a "straw petty bourgeois," as he puts it—by suggesting "that organic farming under capitalism is offered as an alternative to revolutionary struggle. It is 'merely' a struggle for safer food production and better quality food." Organizations such as the Northeast Organic Farming Association, he says, link "small producers, artisans, consumer groups, and innovators in a generally progressive movement in conflict with monopolized agriculture. They have been inventing ways of reducing costs so that the working people of our cities can also get the better quality food they deserve."

But the problem is neither *monopolized* agriculture, nor *monopolized* industry, commerce, or banking: it's *capitalism* and the *capitalist state*. Since the rise of imperialism more than a century ago, "anti-monopoly" politics in the United States has been the politics of capitalist reform. From the Populists of the late 1800s to the U.S. Communist Party's long-standing call for an "anti-monopoly coalition," which guides the politics of their milieu today, the aim has been to channel workers, farmers, and our organizations toward supporting some supposedly "anti-monopoly" wing of bourgeois politics, usually a Democrat. In the run-up to the 2004 U.S. presidential election, the Buchanan/Nader campaign rapprochement, raising money from the same right-wing mailing lists while railing against "big business" and "domination by corporatists," offers a passing example.

After reading Levins's reply, I visited the Web site of the Northeast Organic Farming Association. I was struck by the logo featured on the leaflet for NOFA's August 2004 summer conference: it's a woman guiding a horse-drawn plow. The advertised keynote speaker is Vandana Shiva, a well-known campaigner against genetically modified crops. In a 2003 interview posted on ecoworld.org, Shiva states her opposition to "all systems of modern industrial farming, whether they be the Green Revolution, chemical agriculture or genetic engineering," adding that "industrialization is desacralization" and "a project of hubris." (This foe of industrial hubris, by the way, hails from India, where less than half of some 650,000 rural villages—home to 60 percent of the population—have access to drinkable water or electricity.)

Another thing that caught my eye is NOFA's "Raw Milk Campaign," aimed at repealing government bans on sales of nonpasteurized milk. The website hastens to caution "the young, elderly, and individuals with compromised immune systems [to] research and consider carefully the risks and benefits associated with drinking raw milk. . . . As with all whole, living foods, NOFA suggests you know the animal care standards and sanitary practices of your milk producer"—advice few workers have time to pay attention to when grabbing a quart at the supermarket or 7-Eleven on the way home from work!

Levins says organizations such as NOFA "have been inventing ways of reducing costs so that the working people of our cities can also get the better-quality food they deserve." And he closes by saying that "a revolutionary movement has to challenge the destructive, alienating nature of all aspects of capitalist society in order to build the kind of movement that can liberate the working class and the whole of society."

The *Militant* articles are not about building a movement that can "liberate the working class," or ensure it gets something it deserves. They stand on the opening sentence of the rules of the International Working Men's Association, the First International, drafted by Karl Marx one hundred forty years ago: "The emancipation of the working classes must be conquered by the working classes themselves." That is why the issues posed by Richard Levins are important to discuss. Without clarity on them, there can be no worker-farmer alliance solid enough to achieve that goal.

TWO FINAL COMMENTS

Richard Levins replies

Steve Clark's response to my advocacy of ecological agriculture offers a kindergarten-level lesson in historical materialism, a criticism of Vandana Shiva, references to genetically engineered organisms, and episodes from Russian history, but does not address the major points of contention:

1. Under capitalism, knowledge is created and adopted to meet the needs of the capitalist class: maximum profit and control over the labor force. The capitalists apply criteria of "efficiency" which value the benefits to themselves while as much of the cost as possible is dumped on the present and future working class as "externalities."

2. When the working class comes to power it has the opportunity and necessity to develop its own relations with nature, evaluating world science and choosing research directions and technologies that are productive, protect the health of the producers and of the whole population, and are sustainable and supportive of the new social relations. Therefore technological progress is not along a single pathway but can go in different directions. We always have to ask, progress for whom?

3. Ecological methods in agriculture including pest control and promoting soil fertility have been demonstrated to be productive, economical, and socially and biologically sustainable. Therefore Cuba, after experiencing the approach of the "green revolution," is moving along this pathway. The emergency of the Special Period accelerated the process, but it is a long-term direction.

Steve Clark comments

1. As Richard Levins notes, the points on social labor, the mode of production, commodity fetishism, and the transformation of nature in my rejoinder may well be kindergarten level. What I addressed was the fact that his reply to the *Militant* series repeatedly flunked that kindergarten test.

2. It was Levins who, as his only concrete example of "the organic movement" in the United States, pointed to the Northeast Organic Farming Association as a "generally progressive movement in conflict with monopolized agriculture." My rejoinder noted that Vandana Shiva, a self-described foe of "all systems of modern industrial farming," was invited by NOFA to be the keynote speaker at its 2004 conference; that the conference logo is a horse-drawn plow; and that the group campaigns to repeal laws requiring pasteurization of milk. In what class framework can such positions be defined as progressive? "Anti-monopoly" politics can be, and often are, the umbrella under which "left" and "right" make common cause—to the deadly peril of the working class, as the history of the twentieth century amply proves.

3. Levins's reply to the *Militant* articles explained in some detail his opposition to the development and use of genetically modified organisms. The rejoinder, like the initial articles in the *Militant*, presented the view that the risks inherent in this developing technology can be controlled and its advantages harnessed for the benefit of humanity. It's a class question. And the road taken by Cuba's toilers points the way.

4. What Levins passes off as mere "episodes in Russian history" are in fact the record of more than six decades during which a privileged caste, and the international Stalinist movement it dominated, combined murderous

violence with a counterfeit of Marxism to carry out a counterrevolutionary assault against those determined to continue Lenin's proletarian internationalist course. The result, time and again, was bloody defeats and setbacks to struggles by working people and oppressed nations worldwide. Despite Levins's dismissive view, educating and organizing revolutionary-minded workers, farmers, and youth to understand why those events occurred and thus minimize the odds that such "episodes" are ever again repeated is far from secondary for science or society. The future of humanity depends on it.

5. As to Levins's "major points of contention," these have not been issues of disagreement. The one exception is the argument implied in the last of his three points, which presupposes that the use by farmers (in Cuba or elsewhere) of chemical fertilizers, pesticides, and herbicides cannot be "productive, economical, and socially and biologically sustainable." The *Militant* series and rejoinder argue against the categorical exclusion of any technology or scientific advance available to the toilers. The root of the often devastating consequences of capitalist methods of industrial farming cannot be reduced to synthetic inputs, transgenic crops, the use of machinery, or any other specific tool. Instead, the source is the way in which all such instruments of production are deployed by the exploiters, whether in field or factory, in their competition to accumulate capital.

Until the proletariat and its allies free the organization of social labor and its transformation of nature from the constraints of private property in the means of production, science and technology will continue to be put to use by the exploiters to ensure reproduction of the social relations that maintain their wealth and class rule, regardless of the effects on workers and farmers, or on the earth's atmosphere, soil, and waters. Once freed of those constraints, the productive possibilities open to humanity are beyond our ability today even to imagine. As Marx emphasized one hundred and fifty years ago, the point is for working people and their allies *to change* those class relations. That is the proletarian answer to the question quite rightly posed by Richard Levins: "Progress for whom?" But it can only be answered practically, and by simultaneously answering the always intertwined question: "By whom?"

New International

A MAGAZINE OF MARXIST POLITICS AND THEORY

NEW INTERNATIONAL NO. 12
CAPITALISM'S LONG HOT WINTER HAS BEGUN

Jack Barnes

and "Their Transformation and Ours," Resolution of the Socialist Workers Party
Today's accelerating global capitalist crisis—the opening stages of what will be decades of economic, financial, and social convulsions and class battles—accompanies a continuation of the most far-reaching shift in Washington's military policy and organization since the US buildup toward World War II. Class-struggle-minded working people must face this historic turning point for imperialism, and draw satisfaction from being "in their face" as we chart a revolutionary course to confront it. $16. Also in Spanish, French, Swedish, and Arabic.

NEW INTERNATIONAL NO. 14
REVOLUTION, INTERNATIONALISM, AND SOCIALISM: THE LAST YEAR OF MALCOLM X

Jack Barnes

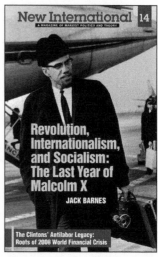

In addition to the lead article, "The Last Year of Malcolm X," this issue contains "The Clintons' Antilabor Legacy: Roots of the 2008 World Financial Crisis." Jack Barnes explains how the Clinton administration, and both Republican and Democratic administrations before it, stepped up assaults on working people and, at the same time, helped bring on the massive mortgage, household, corporate, and government debts that are by-products of today's world crisis of capitalist production. The results for workers and farmers worldwide are devastating.

Also in No. 14: "The Stewardship of Nature Also Falls to the Working Class"; *and* "Setting the Record Straight on Fascism and World War II." $14. Also in Spanish, French, and Swedish.

NEW INTERNATIONAL NO. 11

U.S. IMPERIALISM HAS LOST THE COLD WAR

Jack Barnes

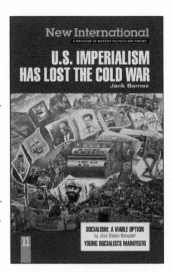

Contrary to imperialist expectations at the opening of the 1990s in the wake of the collapse of regimes across Eastern Europe and the USSR claiming to be communist, the workers and farmers there have not been crushed. The toilers remain an intractable obstacle to imperialism's advance, one the exploiters will have to confront in class battles and war. $16. Also in Spanish, French, Swedish, and Icelandic.

NEW INTERNATIONAL NO. 8

CHE GUEVARA, CUBA, AND THE ROAD TO SOCIALISM

Articles by Ernesto Che Guevara, Carlos Rafael Rodríguez, Carlos Tablada, Mary-Alice Waters, Steve Clark, Jack Barnes

Exchanges from the opening years of the Cuban Revolution and today on the political perspectives defended by Guevara as he helped lead working people to advance the transformation of economic and social relations in Cuba. $10. Also in Spanish.

NEW INTERNATIONAL NO. 5

THE COMING REVOLUTION IN SOUTH AFRICA

Jack Barnes

Writing a decade before the white supremacist regime fell, Barnes explores the social roots of apartheid in South African capitalism and tasks of urban and rural toilers in dismantling it, as they forge a communist leadership of the working class. $14. Also in Spanish and French.

INDEX

A

Africa, 3, 19, 32, 34, 51, 145–46, 155; electrification in, 3, 30, 139; immigration from, 46–47, 52–53; imperialist exploitation of, 42–43, 95, 139–40, 195

Agribusiness, 136, 151–55, 156, 196, 197

Agriculture, 57, 169–70, 185–86; advances in, 141–42, 169–70, 176; capitalism and, 141–45, 150–51, 195; Stalinist policies, 188–90, 193. *See also* Cuban agriculture; Farmers; Organic farming

Albania, 71

Algeria, 79, 80–81

Alliance for Progress, 30

America's Road to Socialism (Cannon), 32

Anarchists, 148

Anti-Ballistic Missile Treaty, 88, 89

"Antimonopoly" politics, 200–201, 204

Anti–Vietnam War movement, 63

Argentina, 30, 34, 43–44, 149

Asia, 19, 32, 34, 51, 87–88, 155; electrification in, 3, 29, 30, 139; immigration from, 46–47, 52–

53; imperialist exploitation of, 42, 95, 139–40, 195

Australia, 29, 42, 53, 139

Azerbaijan, 79

B

Banking system, 87–88, 152–53, 154, 200; and imperialism, 43–45

Bell Curve, The (Herrnstein and Murray), 48

Ben Bella, Ahmed, 79, 80

Bishop, Maurice, 72, 78, 79, 120

Blacks, 57, 60–65, 66

Blair, Anthony, 87

Bolshevik Party, 24, 95, 120, 192; international perspective of, 17–18, 67, 68, 119–20; and Marxist continuity, 115–16, 119. *See also* Worker-Bolsheviks

Borroto, Carlos, 197–98

Brazil, 30, 34, 149

Brezhnev, Leonid, 176, 192, 193

Buchanan, Patrick, 46, 49, 50, 201

Buffenbarger, Tom, 101–2

Buffet, Warren, 49

Burkina Faso, 79, 81, 120, 145–46

Bush, George W., 44, 84, 88–91, 101, 108

CLASS STRUGGLE IN THE UNITED STATES

Is Socialist Revolution in the U.S. Possible?
A Necessary Debate

MARY-ALICE WATERS

In two talks, presented as part of a wide-ranging debate at the Venezuela International Book Fairs in 2007 and 2008, Waters explains why a socialist revolution in the United States is possible. Why revolutionary struggles by working people are inevitable, forced upon us by the crisis-driven assaults of the propertied classes. As solidarity grows among a fighting vanguard of working people, the outlines of coming class battles can already be seen. $7. Also in Spanish, French, and Swedish.

Cuba and the Coming American Revolution

JACK BARNES

The Cuban Revolution of 1959 had a worldwide political impact, including on working people and youth in the imperialist heartland. As the mass, proletarian-based struggle for Black rights was already advancing in the US, the social transformation fought for and won by the Cuban toilers set an example that socialist revolution is not only necessary—it can be made and defended.

This second edition, with a new foreword by Mary-Alice Waters, should be read alongside *Is Socialist Revolution in the U.S. Possible?* $10. Also in Spanish and French.

The Cuban Five

The Cuban Five
Who They Are
Why They Were Framed
Why They Should Be Free

Presents the facts on the worldwide struggle to free Gerardo Hernández, Ramón Labañino, Antonio Guerrero, Fernando González, and René González. Shows how this battle to defend the Five is part of the class struggle in the US, where millions of working people know how the courts and prisons are used to punish those who refuse to accept the conditions imposed on us by capitalism. $5. Also in Spanish and French.

Cuba and Angola
Fighting for Africa's Freedom and Our Own

The story of Cuba's nearly 16-year internationalist mission to aid the people of Angola, in the words of those who made that history, including Fidel Castro, Nelson Mandela, and Raúl Castro. With a special feature by Gabriel García Márquez. Also includes accounts by three of the Cuban Five who fought in Angola. $12. Also in Spanish.

www.pathfinderpress.com

"One of the ways our revolution will be judged in years to come is by how well we have solved the problems facing women."

FIDEL CASTRO, 1974

Women in Cuba:
The Making of a Revolution
Within the Revolution

Vilma Espín
Asela de los Santos
Yolanda Ferrer

$20

Women and Revolution:
The Living Example of the
Cuban Revolution

Asela de los Santos
Mary-Alice Waters

$7

As working people in Cuba fought to bring down a bloody tyranny in the 1950s, the unprecedented integration of women in the ranks and leadership of the struggle was not an aberration. It was intertwined with the proletarian course of the leadership of the Cuban Revolution from the start.

Women in Cuba: The Making of a Revolution Within the Revolution is the story of that revolution and how it transformed the women and men who made it. The book was introduced at the 2012 Havana International Book Fair by a panel of speakers from Cuba and the US.

Women and Revolution: The Living Example of the Cuban Revolution contains the presentations from that event.

Both titles also in Spanish.

50 YEARS OF COVERT OPERATIONS IN THE US

Washington's political police and the American working class
Larry Seigle, Farrell Dobbs, Steve Clark

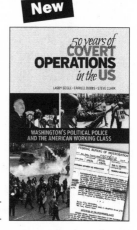

New

The 15-year political campaign of the Socialist Workers Party to expose decades of spying and disruption by the FBI and other federal cop agencies targeting working-class organizations and other opponents of government policies. Traces the origins of bipartisan efforts to expand presidential powers and build the "national security" state essential to maintaining capitalist rule. Includes "Imperialist War and the Working Class" by Farrell Dobbs. $12. Also in Spanish.

SOCIALISM ON TRIAL

New Edition

Testimony at Minneapolis Sedition Trial
James P. Cannon

The revolutionary program of the working class, as presented during the 1941 trial—on the eve of US entry into World War II—of leaders of the Minneapolis labor movement and the Socialist Workers Party on frame-up charges of "seditious conspiracy." Includes Cannon's answer to ultraleft critics of his testimony, drawing lessons from Marx and Engels to the October 1917 revolution in Russia and beyond. $16. Also in Spanish.

www.pathfinderpress.com

New from Pathfinder!

"I will die the way I've lived"
15 watercolors by Antonio Guerrero for the 15th anniversary of the imprisonment of the Cuban Five

Fifteen paintings that graphically portray the 17 months the Cuban Five spent in the "hole" at the Federal Detention Center in Miami, following their arrest in 1998. A window through which workers everywhere can identify with the battles waged by the Five, and appreciate not only their integrity, courage, and creativity but also their sense of humor. $7. Also in Spanish.

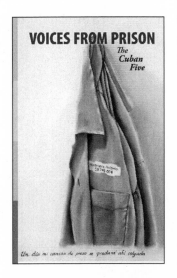

Voices from Prison: The Cuban Five

The revolutionary integrity, strength, and humanity of the Five come through in the voices heard here. Above all, we see the respect they have won for themselves among other prisoners. And why the same happens among working people everywhere who have experienced in their own lives the effects of capitalist "justice." $7. Also in Spanish.

www.pathfinderpress.com

EXPAND Your Revolutionary Library

The Working Class and the Transformation of Learning
The Fraud of Education Reform under Capitalism
JACK BARNES

"Until society is reorganized so that education is a human activity from the time we are very young until the time we die, there will be no education worthy of working, creating humanity." $3. Also in Spanish, French, Swedish, Icelandic, Farsi, and Greek.

Puerto Rico: Independence Is a Necessity
RAFAEL CANCEL MIRANDA

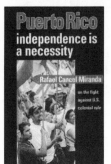

In two interviews, one of five Puerto Rican Nationalists imprisoned by Washington for more than 25 years until 1979 speaks out on the brutal reality of US colonial domination, the campaign to free Puerto Rican political prisoners, the example of Cuba's socialist revolution, and the ongoing struggle for independence. $6. Also in Spanish.

We Are Heirs of the World's Revolutions
Speeches from the Burkina Faso Revolution 1983–87
THOMAS SANKARA

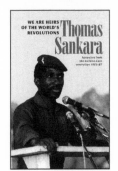

How peasants and workers in this West African country established a popular revolutionary government and began to fight hunger, illiteracy and economic backwardness imposed by imperialist domination, and the oppression of women inherited from class society. They set an example not only for workers and small farmers in Africa, but those the world over. $10. Also in Spanish and French.

Thomas Sankara Speaks
The Burkina Faso Revolution 1983–87

Led by Sankara, the revolutionary government of Burkina Faso in West Africa set an electrifying example. Peasants, workers, women, and youth mobilized to carry out literacy and immunization drives; to sink wells, plant trees, build dams, erect housing; to combat women's oppression and transform exploitative relations on the land; to free themselves from the imperialist yoke and solidarize with others engaged in that fight internationally. $24. Also in French.

Maurice Bishop Speaks
The Grenada Revolution and Its Overthrow, 1979–83

The triumph of the 1979 revolution in the Caribbean island of Grenada had "importance for all struggles around the world," said Maurice Bishop, its central leader. Invaluable lessons from that workers and farmers government, overturned in a Stalinist-led coup in 1983, can be found in this collection. $25

The Jewish Question
A Marxist Interpretation
ABRAM LEON

Traces the historical rationalizations of anti-Semitism to the fact that, in the centuries preceding the domination of industrial capitalism, Jews emerged as a "people-class" of merchants, moneylenders, and traders. Leon explains why the propertied rulers incite renewed Jew-hatred in the epoch of capitalism's decline. $22

WOMEN'S LIBERATION & SOCIALISM

Cosmetics, Fashions, and the Exploitation of Women

JOSEPH HANSEN, EVELYN REED,
MARY-ALICE WATERS

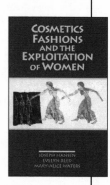

How big business plays on women's second-class status and social insecurities to market cosmetics and rake in profits. The introduction by Mary-Alice Waters explains how the entry of millions of women into the workforce during and after World War II irreversibly changed US society and laid the basis for a renewed rise of struggles for women's emancipation. $15

Woman's Evolution

From Matriarchal Clan to Patriarchal Family

EVELYN REED

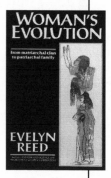

Assesses women's leading and still largely unknown contributions to the development of human civilization and refutes the myth that women have always been subordinate to men. "Certain to become a classic text in women's history"—*Publishers Weekly.* $32

Abortion Is a Woman's Right!

PAT GROGAN, EVELYN REED

Why abortion rights are central not only to the fight for the full emancipation of women, but to forging a united and fighting labor movement. $6. Also in Spanish.

Communist Continuity and the Fight for Women's Liberation

Documents of the Socialist Workers Party 1971–86

How did the oppression of women begin? Who benefits? What social forces have the power to end women's second-class status? 3 volumes, edited with preface by Mary-Alice Waters. $30

CULTURE AND POLITICS

ART AND REVOLUTION
WRITINGS ON LITERATURE, POLITICS, AND CULTURE
Leon Trotsky

One of the outstanding revolutionary leaders of the 20th century examines the place and aesthetic autonomy of art, literature, and artistic expression in the struggle for a new, socialist society. $22

SOCIALISM AND MAN IN CUBA

Ernesto Che Guevara, Fidel Castro

Guevara's best-known presentation of the political tasks and challenges in leading the transition from capitalism to socialism. Includes Castro's 1987 speech on the 20th anniversary of Guevara's death. $7. Also in Spanish, French, and Swedish.

JOHN COLTRANE & THE JAZZ REVOLUTION OF THE 1960s

Frank Kofsky

An account of John Coltrane's role in spearheading innovations in jazz that were an expression of the new cultural and political ferment that marked the rise of the mass struggle for Black rights. $30

THEIR MORALS AND OURS
THE CLASS FOUNDATIONS OF MORAL PRACTICE
Leon Trotsky

Participating in the revolutionary workers movement "with open eyes and an intense will—only this can give the highest moral satisfaction to a thinking being," Trotsky writes. He explains how morality is rooted in the interests of contending social classes. With a reply by the pragmatist philosopher John Dewey and a Marxist response to Dewey by George Novack. $15

The Russian Revolution

The History of the Russian Revolution
LEON TROTSKY

The social, economic, and political dynamics of the first socialist revolution as told by one of its central leaders. How, under Lenin's leadership, the Bolshevik Party led the overturn of the monarchist regime of the landlords and capitalists and brought to power a government of the workers and peasants. Unabridged, 3 vols. in one. $38. Also in Russian.

The Revolution Betrayed
What Is the Soviet Union and Where Is It Going?
LEON TROTSKY

In 1917 the working class and peasantry of Russia carried out one of the most profound revolutions in history. Yet within ten years a political counterrevolution by a privileged social layer whose chief spokesperson was Joseph Stalin was being consolidated. This classic study of the Soviet workers state and its degeneration illuminates the roots of the social and political crisis in Russia and other countries that formerly made up the Soviet Union. $20. Also in Spanish.

The First Five Years of the Communist International
LEON TROTSKY

During its first five years, the Communist International, guided by V.I. Lenin, Leon Trotsky, and other central Bolshevik leaders, sought to build a world movement of Communist Parties capable of leading the toilers to overthrow capitalist exploitation and colonial oppression. This two-volume collection contains Trotsky's speeches and writings from the first four Comintern congresses. Volume 1, $28; volume 2, $29.

WWW.PATHFINDERPRESS.COM

Unions Their past, present, and future

Trade Unions in the Epoch of Imperialist Decay

Leon Trotsky, Farrell Dobbs, Karl Marx

Food for thought—and action—from revolutionary leaders of three different generations of the modern working-class movement. Invaluable to the practical education of militant workers relearning today what a strike is and how it can be fought and won. $16

The Eastern Airlines Strike

ACCOMPLISHMENTS OF THE RANK-AND-FILE MACHINISTS

Ernie Mailhot, Judy Stranahan, Jack Barnes

The story of the 686-day strike in which a rank-and-file resistance by Machinists prevented Eastern's union-busting onslaught from becoming the road toward a profitable nonunion airline. $12

The 1985–86 Hormel Meat-Packers Strike in Austin, Minnesota

Fred Halstead

The hard-fought strike against Hormel opened a round of battles by packinghouse workers that—together with strikes by paper workers, cannery workers, and western coal miners—marked a break in the rout of US unions that began during the 1981–82 recession. $6. Also in Spanish.

Labor's Giant Step

THE FIRST TWENTY YEARS OF THE CIO: 1936–55

Art Preis

The story of the explosive labor struggles and political battles in the 1930s that built the industrial unions. And how those unions became the vanguard of a mass social movement that began transforming US society. $30

www.pathfinderpress.com

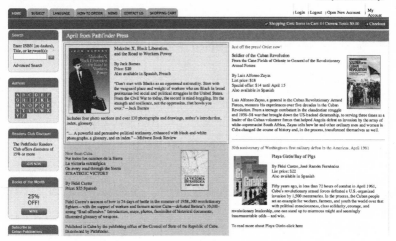

National liberation socialism

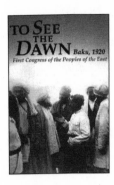

To See the Dawn
Baku, 1920—First Congress of the Peoples of the East

How can peasants and workers in the colonial world throw off imperialist exploitation? By what means can working people overcome national, religious, and other divisions incited by their own ruling classes and act together for their common class interests? These questions were addressed by 2,000 delegates to the 1920 Congress of the Peoples of the East. $24

Workers of the World and Oppressed Peoples, Unite!
Proceedings and Documents of the Second Congress of the Communist International, 1920

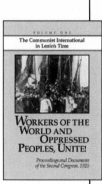

The debate among delegates from 37 countries takes up key questions of working-class strategy and program—the fight for national liberation, the revolutionary transformation of trade unions, the worker-farmer alliance, participation in elections and parliament, and the structure and tasks of Communist Parties. The reports, resolutions, and debates offer a vivid portrait of social struggles in the era of the Bolshevik-led October Revolution. Two volumes. $65

Questions of National Policy and Proletarian Internationalism
V.I. LENIN

Why the fight of oppressed nations for self-determination is decisive in the worldwide proletarian struggle to take and hold power. Why workers and farmers in imperialist countries have a deep class interest in championing this right. $16

WWW.PATHFINDERPRESS.COM

NEW INTERNATIONAL AROUND THE WORLD

New International is also published in Spanish as
Nueva Internacional and French as **Nouvelle Internationale**.
Selected issues are available in Swedish as **Ny International**
and in Icelandic as **Nýtt Alþóðlegt**. All are distributed
worldwide by Pathfinder Press.

AVAILABLE AT
WWW.PATHFINDERPRESS.COM
and at the following locations

United States
(and Caribbean, Latin America, and East Asia):
Pathfinder Books, 306 W. 37th St., 13th Floor
New York, NY 10018

Canada
Pathfinder Books, 7107 St. Denis, Suite 204
Montreal, QC H2S 2S5

United Kingdom
(and Europe, Africa, Middle East, and South Asia):
Pathfinder Books, First Floor, 120 Bethnal Green Road
(entrance in Brick Lane), London E2 6DG

Australia
(and Southeast Asia and the Pacific)
Pathfinder, Level 1, 3/281-287 Beamish St., Campsie, NSW 2194
Postal address: P.O. Box 164, Campsie, NSW 2194

New Zealand
Pathfinder, 188a Onehunga Mall, Onehunga, Auckland 1061
Postal address: P.O. Box 3025, Auckland 1140